FIND YOUR W[illegible]!

Find your why™

To Become Frickin' Awesome

By

Cheryl Chapman

& Marion Bevington

Orders: Please go to www.cheryl-chapman.com
ISBN: 978-0-9934587-1-2

First published 2015

Printed in the U.K. for The Find Your WHY! Foundation by Printdomain Ltd 107 High St, Thurnscoe, Rotherham S63 0QZ

CONTENTS

ACKNOWLEGEMENTS

Thank you to my parents, who gave me the opportunity to experience life, who loved me and kept me safe.

Thank you to my sister Gemma (I was an only child for 15 years and 11 months and then you arrived and my inheritance halved – family joke thank you for being there for me and providing me with an amazing nephew Leon (who will be a professional footballer – watch this space).

To my husband Mr C, my rock, who has always supported me by allowing me to follow my WHY! You are one in a million – Love You.

A special mention to My Staffordshire Bull Terrier 'Ozzy Dog', who sat a my feet whilst I wrote these words.

To Marion who helped me to become carefree, you are my friend teacher and guide. You are frickin'awesome (and very intelligent).

Finally, Thank you to **YOU**, that's right YOU. You know who you are You played a big part of my life by either supporting me, pushing me inspiring me and sometimes even pissing me off (I now know that was because I let you). I hope that you are happy and living your WHY!

And from Marion...

I'm so grateful to my many teachers, some have led me to wisdom with explicit positive lessons of sharing and practice; and others are my teachers because they really push my (negative) buttons!

I want to say a huge thank you to Cheryl Chapman, who is both types of teacher to me. Cheryl, you have been a huge influence on me since 2012 when we began our friendship, you see in me something that I cannot see in myself, and you do so with a deep appreciation. You've inspired me to keep being myself even when don't know what that means! Your support, love and constant faith in me have allowed me to grow in confidence, able to share my story my gifts and my stardust – Thank you Cheryl words are not enough.

“You were created for something awesome. Find your WHY!”

PREFACE

This book is based on 9 Points of Wisdom:

Point 1

You are the only person who can control the way you feel.

Blaming others for how you feel is giving away your power – making you a passive victim. By learning how to respond, and not react, you can take back your power and become actively responsible for YOU. This will allow you to take control of yourself and your feelings.

Point 2

You can't change anyone else.

Become aware of things that you cannot change, such as other people's opinions and behaviour. If people are beyond your influence then don't waste your energy. No matter how hard you try, they won't change.

You can be the juiciest, ripest cherry possible, but the reality is that some people will always hate cherries.

Point 3

Your past is your past.

All of the pain, frustration and sadness that you have experienced in your life has brought you to the place where you are now, and made you the person we see today. These experiences have shaped you and served you.

You can choose to keep living in the past, or move forward towards your future.

Point 4

You are what you think.

Whether you are a sister, brother, daughter, son, friend, lover, wife, husband, mother, father grandmother or grandfather – you have thoughts. Energy goes where attention flows. Thoughts become words, words become behaviour, behaviours become habits, habits become values and values become destiny.

Surround yourselves with others that want the same things as you.

Point 5

Before you start your journey, you need to know where you are now.

Just like a satellite navigation system in a car, you need to know where your starting point is before any journey can begin. Discovering where you are consciously, and unconsciously, will help you to pinpoint your current life location.

Point 6

You must be clear on what it is that you want.

One day you will die – FACT!

You must decide what you want to happen in your life – don't leave it to chance.

The difference between successful people and unsuccessful people, is that successful people KNOW what they want, and go after it! Unsuccessful people do not and so they end up where life takes them – like a leaf blowing in the wind – directionless.

Point 7

You can have the life you want, but you have to take action.

The Law Of Attraction has two equally important parts. The first part is the ability to attract, and the 2nd part is that you NEED to take action. As Einstein once said, "Insanity isn't doing the same thing every day, it's doing the same thing every day and expecting something to change."

If you change nothing, nothing changes.

Point 8

You need to **FIND YOUR WHY**.

Without a **WHY** life will just happen to you, you'll die with regrets.

When you **FIND YOUR WHY**, you'll be motivated, full of energy, satisfied, happy and fulfilled.

You will be a role model to others and inspire them to find their **WHY** too. This is the purpose of your life, the reason **WHY** you are on this planet.

Here's the thing to help you **FIND YOUR WHY**, there is another very important question to answer and that is **WHY** are you where you are right now?

If you don't answer this vital question nothing will change in your life and let's be honest you did not pick up this book because everything is rosy in your life right now, right?

And so to finding what is not working for you right now, will help you to know what changes are needed in your life to make a positive impact in your life

Point 9

You can make these changes, even if right now you don't know how. In this book, we will provide you with a plan. This plan will help you to take back control of your life, so that you can LIVE – LOVE – LAUGH every day; all in your own unique way.

If you can see and feel a connection with any of these Points of Wisdom, now is the time to invest in yourself and begin the next chapter of your life.

Additionally, if you know anyone within your network of friends and family who might also be interested in these points of wisdom, please let them know so they too can benefit from the content of this life-changing book.

With love,

Cheryl & Marion

Cheryl Chapman   Marion Bevington

But before we begin our journey together, there is something I think you might want to know ...

CHERYL'S WHY!

It's November 2013 and I'm lying on my back in the middle of a room in Angel Islington. It's been over 40 minutes, and I can hear my stomach rumbling.

Leaning over me, I can see her fiddling with her papers and workbook. The room is filled with every kind of clutter. A hammock, hand drawn etchings on the wall, piles of books and foreign trinkets; you name it she's got it. She is the female version of Indiana Jones, in search of a thousand ancient truths.

As she speaks, it's like Cilla Black has arrived in the room, "Ok Cheryl, put your hand up and try to resist. Mmmm…yes. Ok, and again."

As I watch her in her flowing orange, white and burgundy hippy frock, she drops some papers on the floor, and as her red glasses slip to the end of her nose, I can't help thinking, "Bless her – I don't think she's mastered this yet, but she's a friend and she asked me to help her. I'll just lie here I'm sure it will all be over soon."

Little did I know what was about to happen…

"Ok Cheryl, with the information I'm picking up on, it is either you have to watch the energy you give to others

(As she is pointing to her book, I'm thinking, "This is a crock of shit!") Or, it's you have to be careful?"

"OH MY GOD, THEY'VE FOUND OUT!" The voice in my head is loud and scared. My stomach starts to somersault. Finally, the tears start to flow. My mind goes back to when I was 5 years old, "But WHY, Mummy?"

This is where it all started.

CHAPTER 1

CAN YOU KEEP A SECRET?

Can you remember a time when you were a child?

Can you remember the questions you used to ask all the time?

Why? Why? Why?

Why are there stars in the sky?

Why is the sun yellow?

But why do I have to wear this pink dress?

That's right, a child's most used word is WHY!

If you'd been with me in October 1969, you would have witnessed a time when that question was the number one thing on my mind.

Picture the scene. I'm standing in an army quarter hallway. My mother, swinging sixties high hair and short skirt, is wrapping a silver chain around my neck. On the end of it is a key.

"Can you keep a secret, Cheryl? Mummy needs you to keep a secret. You can't tell anyone about this key – I need you to keep it hidden until you come home and then use it to let yourself in, can you do this for Mummy?"

"But why, Mummy?"

"Cheryl, Daddy is away with the other soldiers and Mummy needs to work at the TV Station, so I won't be here when you come home. But you're a big girl now, so you will be fine until I get back. Remember you've got to be careful, don't tell anyone. Don't let anyone in, or Mummy might get into trouble and you might not see her again."

At first it was fine. I would run around the flat, bounce on the settee and eat as much ice cream as I wanted. But when it got dark I would hide under the blanket on my bed, praying my mummy would come home soon. The reality was that I was only on my own for about an hour. However, I'm sure you would agree an hour for a child feels like a long time.

I'd like to tell you that this was the only time I was asked to wear the key. Unfortunately this happened almost every day, from the age of 5, throughout my childhood. Have you ever thought about how your upbringing influences your adult life? For me it wasn't until I got older that some other elements of being an 'army brat' started to appear.

Me & my mum (I told you her skirt was short)

Are you a Gypsy?

It's August 2011 and I'm sitting with my friend Toria (she looks like Angelina Jolie) in Bettys Tea Room in York, England. Bettys is one of those quintessentially British establishments that is steeped in history and has been around since 1919.

Personally, I love it for the heart shape cakes.

"So Chez, (that's what all my friends call me) how's the job?"

"Oh you know, same shit – different day, I think it's time for a move!"

Looking at her watch, Toria says, "Oh yeah that will be about right, you've been there 2 years and so this is when you get itchy feet. Why do you think you constantly want to move? Are you a gypsy?"

With a dismissive tone, I start to recall the list of jobs that I've had recently. I started enthusiastically imagining she's got it wrong – only to find out she's right …22 months, 24 months, 2 years and nearly 2 years again!

"Well Toria, it's because my dad was in the army. We used to move every 2 years – clearly it's in my blood. Besides, sometimes I just don't feel like I fit in."

"Chez, maybe you should have a change in your career instead of just moving from one place to another, experiencing the same problems? For someone who thinks they don't fit in, you're great with people. Maybe you should consider being a counsellor?"

"You are joking right? I'm too old to make any changes now. I've been working in retail for over 25 years, how the hell could I do anything different?"

I also had a secret that I couldn't let anyone know about.

My bestfriends

Maybe it was because I couldn't get excited about my job, or maybe because my husband was away from home a lot...whatever it was, I found myself spending every weekend with two of my favourite friends: Gordon & Stella.

Let me tell you about Gordon and Stella. Gordon had wide shoulders and a white cap, and a way of helping me feel numb. Stella... well, she supported me through the tough times by making me feel feisty. Together, they had the ability to help me forget all my troubles. That's right, if you haven't guessed it by now – I was a binge drinker, with a terrible 'thank god it's Friday' habit. Friday evening began with Gordon's Gin and tins of Stella Artois, and didn't end until the hangover kicked in the next morning. Sometimes it didn't end till Saturday night or Sunday morning.

It was when Monday arrived that the sober truth became apparent. I felt trapped. Trapped in a job I hated, trapped by the debt that I'd accrued as

I bought things designed to make me feel better, to distract me from the reality of the life I'd created. I hated my life. I was fat, frumpy and heading towards 50. I was living a lie. And worse still, I believed there was nothing that could be done.

Then, in October 2011, something happened that completely changed my life forever.

Recruiting for my funeral

If you had been with me on the 15th October 2011, you would have seen me sitting inside The Troxy in London, a large art deco theatre with two sweeping staircases. It was the type of theatre that would have been perfect for the likes of Fred Astaire and Ginger Rogers, but it wasn't dancers that took to the stage that day. On that day, it was speakers.

"Who's this?" said the Indian lady sitting next to me

"Not sure, but he looks small!"

"Ladies and gentlemen, please welcome to the stage... MR ANDY HARRINGTON!"

The audience were clapping and cheering. I wondered if I was in the right place. This was a far cry from my everyday life.

As Andy started his presentation, it was as if he was talking just to me.

"If you were to die tomorrow, who would mourn your loss?"

Turning to the Indian lady next to me, I announced, "Well I've got 43 friends on Facebook, so I guess not many." Then, as if an arrow had been fired into my heart, I heard the words:

"If the number is low, it means you've lead a life of insignificance."

Have you ever had a time when someone spoke to you and you felt like you had a deep connection with them, as if they were on the same wavelength? Well, that was what happened to me that day. So when Andy presented the opportunity to attend the Public Speakers University, I ran straight to the back of the room. I just knew that this guy was going to help me. Maybe you could call it woman's intuition, but whatever it was, I was hooked. After the PSU I was invited to join The Professional Speakers Academy (PSA) and continued to work with Andy as my mentor. I still wasn't really sure what I was doing – but I was certain that it was the right thing.

Back at work, my boss sensed that something was happening...

"Cheryl, it seems like this speaking is of more interest to you than your role here. Your role here should come first, this is how you make a living! You need to choose which you want to carry on with."

Have you ever known with all your heart what you should do, and what the right thing is to do, but before you can do it your head kicks in?

"You have a mortgage to pay, Cheryl. What about all the debt you have, what about your responsibilities?"

I spent the next few days in turmoil. I knew I couldn't speak to my family about it because I didn't want them to worry, so instead I talked to myself.

"What should I do – should I stay on the track that I know so well, with the safety of a salary and a company car, or should I change direction and choose a life that could give me a purpose?"

What would you do?

It was at that time that a friend from The Professional Speakers Academy asked me if I would be a case study for her Kinesiology course. Marion said it could help me to understand which direction to take. I have to admit I didn't really understand what it was, but by now I was desperate!

You have to be careful

Let's return to Angel Islington. There I was, lying on my back, with tears streaming down my face.

"Cheryl, does "you have to be careful" mean something to you?"

"Yes, Marion it does – I understand now that I've tried to be careful all my life. I've tried to do what's best for everyone else, but so far this has just led to me being unhappy and feeling like I don't fit in. But if I'm not careful, what do I do? I've spent my whole life being careful, 43 *fucking* years of being careful!"

It was with Marion's help that I began to see that there was an alternative way to live my life. And so I resigned from my job to follow my purpose, to find my WHY.

It was tough at first. My family thought I'd gone mad. I lost my salary overnight, and my financial situation was dire to say the least.

However, it suddenly felt like I'd got my life back. I felt motivated, and had the time and the energy to make a complete change in direction.

However, I still had those questions like "Am I good enough" so I studied hard in the areas of Life Coaching, Neuro Linguistic Programming and I attended as many motivational events as I could to gain new knowledge. I found my Genetic S.T.Y.L.E Blueprint (the essence of who I really was) and this meant that I was able to see things (no not dead people!) I could identify what was missing in other people's lives and that I could help them to logically change aspects of their lives and business to gain success. Using all these new skills I coached thousands of business owners and individuals to stand up and speak out for my mentor Andy Harrington (I'm sure like me you like to give back to those who have helped you along the way, right?)

However, the truth was I was helping others to create successful businesses and yet I was still working for someone else!

In 2015 Marion (that's right the female Indiana Jones) and I joined together to create The Find Your WHY! Foundation and with her 20 year plus expertise and my new found skills and corporate business experience we help others, like you:

To Find Your WHY! To become (even more) frickin' awesome.

Our client base started to grow, and as we shared more and more success with them, my confidence began to grow too. I used to think I didn't fit in. I used to think that I was the only one who felt so lost, who wondered if this is all there is to life, but now I know that I was not alone. So many women live like that, and now we can help them to choose a life of freedom. I know what it's like to feel trapped, and I wouldn't wish this on anyone else.

Soon we created a place where likeminded women (that we call the WHYs Women) a place where they can collaborate, create and communicate in the community we call The Live Love Laugh Lounge.

In 2016 we started to help WHYs Men too in their own place called The Man Cave.

Without the help of my mentors and guides I wouldn't have even been able to start this journey and so I am so grateful to them. Here's the thing the simple truth is:

"You don't have to figure it out on your own

and

You don't have to do it alone"

I hope that we can support you too.

"The 2 most important days in your life are the day you were born & the day you find ~~out~~ your WHY"

~~Mark Twain~~

Cheryl & Marion

Speaking to an audience in Singapore 2014

Speaking at Queens of Life in Warsaw 2015

Today I travel all over the world sharing a message of hope and help to large groups of people. In the last 2 years I have spoken on stages in Australia, Malaysia, Singapore, Thailand, South Africa, Europe and Canada and The Middle East.

Oh and my funeral got a bit busier with 10,000+ friends on social media!

Appearing on Slovenian TV 2014

I was awarded the Trainer of the Year award by Andy Harrington, the man who helped me to realise I had a gift inside me.

Today I am still renowned as one of the most productive coaches in the World, mentoring thousands of clients internationally.

Joining the Professional Speakers Academy in 2012 and Receiving Trainer of the year award from my mentor Andy Harrington in 2015.

Sharing my WHY! Helping me to win Top Female Speaker in 2016

Cheryl & Marion (The female Indiana Jones).

Why do I do this?

For some reason I'd stopped questioning, and stopped asking "why?" as I got older and just accepted what life gave me. Have you done that too? If so, maybe it's because we were told the answer is, "it's because it just is!"

However, now I believe we should never stop asking. I believe we should never stop trying. Never stop, until you FIND your WHY!

Now you might be thinking what is my WHY!

I believe it is to inspire others to live love and laugh everyday.

So to ensure that I manifest this intention in alignment with my WHY...

I now have A Global Mission

"To Guide 10 Million Disheartened Souls from

WHY Me?
to WHY NOT!"

Live, Love & Laugh every day, By being unique in your own special way.

Cheryl Chapman

Now it's your turn

In the coming chapters, we will reveal how you can go from having a lack of belief in yourself and being easily distracted; to being aware of where you are right now. With our advice, you can set your intentions for the future, and manifest the life you want, by finding your personal WHY.

So let's get started. It's going to be a big dipper of a ride, so fasten yourself in and get ready to scream with excitement!

"We're here to put a dent in the universe Otherwise why else even be here?"

Steve Jobs

CHAPTER 2

HOW TO START A NEW CHAPTER IN YOUR LIFE

There is something that I already know about you (even though you may not be aware of it).

You are unique, precious and one of a kind. For example, think about the probability of you even existing:

1) *Your parents had to meet, they had to have sex and your dad's sperm had to find your mum's egg (I know, too much information!)*
2) *Go further back – both sets of grandparents needed to meet.*
3) *Both sets of great grandparents had to meet theirs & theirs & so on.*
4) *The % chance of you being alive is so small.*
5) *The chance that you would be reading this book right now is even lower.*

We believe that YOU, yes, YOU are here for a reason – a very special reason.

The ups and downs of life can however, certainly take their toll on you, and you may ask yourself, "why am I here?" or, "is this all there is to life?"

Let me ask you, "Why do you get out of bed in the morning?"

Now you may say to earn money, or possibly to take the dog out. Perhaps for you it's more functional, like to have a wee, or maybe you stay in bed till the afternoon?

However you've answered the above, my guess is that it's probably not really about WHY you get out of bed... these are just the things you do, right? But do you know WHY you do them? If this sounds like a difficult question to answer, or maybe even a trick question, don't worry. You're not alone. Just like you, most people don't know what their WHY is or how to find it.

In the following chapters of this book we'll show you how to choose a life of freedom, to live as the real you – authentic, satisfied, fulfilled and knowing why you are here. Knowing your function, as Oprah says. By reading this book, you'll begin to discover exactly what your purpose is as a living being, and how to live your life on your terms and no one else's. It all starts with finding your WHY!

Ok, so you may be thinking, "Cheryl, what do you mean by my WHY?" Allow me to explain...

Your WHY is your purpose, your calling, or you might even say your destiny. It's what inspires and drives you. It is the most important thing in your life, it's what you would fight day and night for, and it should be the motivation behind everything that you do. Unfortunately, so far, there is a good chance that you and many others have lived your lives without even knowing that you should have a WHY. As a result of not having your own WHY, maybe your life is dedicated to someone else's, making someone else's dream come true or helping someone else to achieve their goals.

Well, now it's time to focus on YOU!

This book is designed to help you Find Your WHY. Smile if that sounds like a good idea ☺

Why do you need to find your WHY?

Once you have found your own personal WHY, the world begins to make more sense. You must find it because it is what drives you, gives you energy and pulls your goals towards you. When you find it, it explains everything you do. It effects how you see the world, how you experience it, how you fit in and most importantly of all – it will prove to you that you really are wired for success.

So, you might be thinking, what do we mean 'wired' for success? By this we mean that the wiring in your brain, and in your nervous system, may need to be re-wired to help you if you want to make changes in your life.

STOP! Don't worry, there is no surgery required here (well not the hospital type, anyway!)

Let's explain. There is a feeling part of your brain, called the limbic system, and it knows when something feels right or wrong. Maybe you can remember a time when you just knew that something felt right or wrong?

When you find something that just feels right – it will encourage you, and it will give you energy, inspiration and motivation. It helps you to work in harmony with your brain and your body, and that is why knowing your WHY is crucial for you.

To live without knowing your WHY could mean that you will just exist from day to day, like a fallen leaf from a tree being pushed by an external force, without any control.

Once you have found your WHY, you will know clearly why you do what you do, why you think how you think, why you make the choices you make and why you believe what you believe. Knowing your WHY makes decisions easy to make, because you can base your choices on a simple question – does this fit with my WHY or not?

So, is there a reason why so many follow someone else's WHY instead of their own? Let's take a look at our past to find out. WHY are you where you are right now? It is because you have made a series of decisions that have brought you to here ...buy WHY did you make the decisions you made?

Follow your passion
Stay true to yourself
Never follow
Someone else's path

(Unless you're lost in the woods &
You see a path... in which case follow
that!)

Ellen DeGeneres

The difference between a woman's WHY, and a man's WHY.

Men and women are the poles of humanity – yin and yang. While masculinity is stereotypically expressive, and femininity receptive – they are different and both powerful in their own right.

Are you an AA, an AAA or DD?

Like the positive and negative poles of a battery, both are needed to allow the energy to flow. From one pole the energy flows out, and from the other it flows in. Without both of them the battery would be dead. Humanity is the same. Without the yang of the masculine expressive outwardly focused energy, AND the yin of the feminine receptive inward focused energy, there would be no humanity!

Simply put, a man's WHY generally is about being an individual, standing out, competing, fighting and taking control.

By contrast, a woman is more often about community, being part of a whole, being somebody significant through collaboration, co- operation and helping your own group, community, society or family.

Now although women can be more focused on encouraging all members of the group to become the best that they can be, and being more supportive and less competitive. Sometimes these traits can also lead to women shrinking down and taking only supportive roles. Of course whilst this is a trait, I am not saying that it is black and white. There are some men that care for the community, just as there are some women who care about being an individual and taking control.

This is one of the reasons WHY our retreats are single sex retreats ☺

"Our deepest fear is not that we are inadequate. Our deepest fear is that we are powerful beyond measure. It is our light, not our darkness that most frightens us. We ask ourselves, who am I to be brilliant, gorgeous, talented, fabulous? Actually, who are you not to be? You are a child of God. Your playing small does not serve the world. There is nothing enlightened about shrinking so that other people won't feel insecure around you. We are all meant to shine, as children do. We were born to make manifest the glory of God that is within us. It's not just in some of us; it's in everyone. And as we let our own light shine, we unconsciously give other people permission to do the same. As we are liberated from our own fear, our presence automatically liberates others."

~ Marianne Williamson

Which leads us to ask the following questions:

"What is your WHY?"

"What are you supposed to DO with your life?"

"What are you HERE for?"

"WHY are you where you are?"

At this stage just see if you can answer these questions and then compare them after you have completed the book.

"If just one person says 'because of you I didn't give up!' I know that my WHY has been achieved."

Cheryl Chapman

"IT IS IMPOSSIBLE TO LIVE WITHOUT FAILING AT SOMETHING, UNLESS YOU LIVE SO CAUTIOUSLY THAT YOU MIGHT AS WELL NOT HAVE LIVED AT ALL – IN WHICH CASE YOU FAIL BY DEFAULT."

- J.K.ROWLING

Find your why™

Keep your AIM Straight

- Knowing your WHY helps you to decide what is right for you.

- Be you. You are good enough.

- Trust your intuition/instinct.

- Do what makes you smile.

Question

Do you Love what you do?

CHAPTER 3

HOW DO YOU ACT?

Find out with this quick quiz - I mean every one loves a quiz – right?

1. How do you feel when you wake up on a Monday morning?

a) *I know I have to get up because I can't let others down.*

b) *I hit the snooze button and wish it was Saturday again.*

c) *I feel energised, ready to live life to the full.*

d) *I drag myself into the kitchen, drink my first energy drink and make a strong cup of coffee.*

2. After sharing a great idea with your friend, they tell you they thinks it's a bad idea. What's your reaction?

a) *They're probably right, who do I think I am?*

b) *I wish I'd never told them. Now I feel like a fool!*

c) *I really don't care what they think, I know this is going to be a success.*

d) *I decide to go to the pub and have a drink.*

3. A relationship that you thought was going somewhere special has ended, what are your thoughts?

a) *I guess I wasn't the right person for them.*

b) *Why does this always happen to me?*

c) *As one door closes, another door opens.*

d) *I must call my mates so I can go for a good night out.*

4. What is the number 1 thought that you have in any given day?

a) *How can I make others happy?*

b) *God I'm bored.*

c) *I am so happy and grateful for the life I have.*

d) *What can I eat/drink now?*

5. How would you describe your current situation?

a) *I am constantly busy helping others.*

b) *I feel trapped and unhappy.*

c) *I am living life to the full.*

d) *I am so busy that I have no time for myself.*

6. Where do you see yourself in five years' time?

a) *Wherever the special person in my life is.*

b) *Probably the same place I am now.*

c) *Exactly where my five-year plan is taking me.*

d) *I don't have time to plan.*

7. What do you think about change?

a) *It scares me. You don't know what might happen!*

b) *I can't see anything changing in my life.*

c) *It's what helps me to develop.*

d) *It's frustrating.*

8. Why do you think you're here?

a) *To make others happy.*

b) *To suffer sadness.*

c) *To be happy.*

d) *I don't know where I am.*

Results:

Please add up all your letter scores (A, B, C or D) and then insert your number score in the table below:

A	B	C	D

Mainly A-

You play the role of a people pleaser:

"I'm just a girl or guy who can't say no?"

You tend to put other people's needs before your own.

Potentially, you could be relying on other people's opinions to make decisions in your life.

Concentrating on other people's problems is a way to avoid your own. You are avoiding the pain of being rejected and powerless, when you need to remind yourself that your worth is really much more than what you can ever do for others.

The good news: This book will show you a way to take back your power. By the end of the book you will no longer have to worry about pleasing other people, and you will realise the power of putting yourself before other people. Once you learn to say "NO", things will change for the better and people will have more respect for you; trust me!

Mainly B-

You play the role of a victim.

You tend to think that bad things only happen to you.
Potentially you could be attracting more negativity in your life.
You may be afraid of your own anger, denying it exists, projecting it onto others or waiting for aggression or harm from them. You are highly sensitivity to anger in others, and may even imagine that others have malicious intentions. Your anger is transformed into fear and distrust of others, and into feelings of being hurt or wounded.

The good news: Within this book you will learn how to take back control of yourself, your life and your emotions. By the end of the book you will know how to reconnect to your own feelings, accept them and express them safely. This alone will transform your life and you will realise the power of being your authentic self. Once you learn that you are in charge of your life, you'll never feel like a victim again! Hallelujah

Mainly C-

You play the role of positivity.

You look at the world in a positive light. Potentially, your glass is always half full, but what if your glass gets smashed? If you feel like you have to force yourself to see the positive things in every situation, then you're not allowing yourself to be complete and true to who you are. All emotions are valid. Whether we talk about them or not, they still happen.

The good news: Within this book I will show you how you can use your positivity in a way that will serve you, without eliminating the signs of possible danger. By the end of the book you will have clarity around your life, and find peace in knowing that sometimes you need the lows to appreciate the highs. Once you learn how to accept this, you will be able to live a life full of all emotions. Oh yeah!

Mainly D-

You play the role of the distractor.

You want to keep busy all the time.

You are not aware of how you are really feeling, because you use distracting techniques to keep you busy. This means that you don't have to access your true unresolved emotions. Learning how to resolve those emotions will free you from them, and allow you to focus on what you want rather than avoiding what you don't want.

The good news: Within this book you will learn how to take some time out from distraction. By the end of the book you will be able to appreciate the need for down time and the power of staying focused on one task at a time. Once you learn how to stop your mind from thinking so much, you will be able to complete tasks, and feel great whilst doing so!

So now that you have an idea of where you are starting from, let's begin a new chapter in your life. I am going to help you to improve the areas that are not currently serving you, or maybe even holding you back...

CHAPTER 4

TAKE A.I.M

So you might be thinking, "OK Cheryl & Marion, so I now know that according to your quiz, I'm a people pleaser. I'm a victim, I'm a positive Polly or even a distractor – so what?"

Well, you may be pleased to hear that you are not your behaviour. That's right, YOU are YOU, and your behaviour is something separate altogether. So why is this important? Well it means that you're not a victim or any of the above, even if your behaviour is. Which means that if you make a mistake, it does not make YOU a mistake, do that make sense? In other words you can make a mistake and it doesn't have to affect you or your life – you can learn from it.

For many years I (Cheryl) felt trapped in my life, just thinking, "I guess this is my life, I better get on with it." Then as I started to open my mind to new people, new information and new possibilities, I began to find ways to clear out old beliefs and shift perspectives, Marion helped me work on any blocks that came up and my life changed! After I decided to leave the corporate world, I chose a new direction, where I could use my people skills and the natural skills I had to identify gaps in people's lives / find links in their life that were holding them back. I trained as a Life Coach and studied Neuro Linguistic Programming and I was surprised to find that there were many people who had the same limiting beliefs that I had experienced. Many of the people I worked with had little or no sense of purpose and here's the thing my clients would tell me about other programmes they had invested in that didn't work for them, WHY? Because they became overwhelmed or they didn't think they were worth it. By working with my clients, I was able to help them to identify and overcome these limiting beliefs. I was able to help them create new stories for their future, and to help them find their WHY!

In order to 'Find Your WHY!' there are just 3 areas that you need to master:

1st Area – AWARENESS

Firstly, you need to have **AWARENESS**. So you might be thinking what do we mean by awareness?

Awareness is the ability to see something, to recognise it, to appreciate it and to have some knowledge about something or someone.

In this case we are talking about you having awareness of you in 2 areas of your life.

The 1st step of AWARENESS is to know where you are.

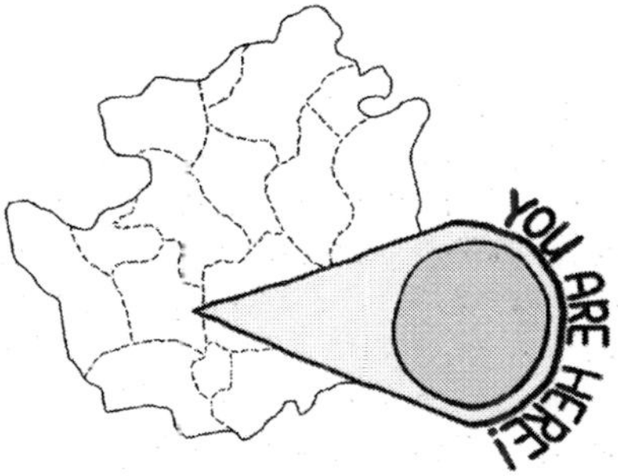

In any journey you have to know where your starting point is

The 2nd step of AWARENESS is knowing why you are where you are right now

Maybe you have recently had a change in your life – check the list below and tick which ones apply to you:

1) Death of a close family or friend
2) Divorce
3) Desertion of children leaving home
4) Disappointment – redundancy, lack of recognition, feeling lonely, a milestone birthday

We call these the 4 D's (no shit Sherlock!) and these areas can send you into a life crisis (sometimes mistaken as a mid-life crisis)

Having AWARENESS is a great starting point in clearing out old beliefs and to help you to identify what might be causing a block, but it isn't everything. You also need to know

2nd Area - INTENTION.

Intention is all about matching your WHY with your goals and ambitions. If you know where you are with awareness, then INTENTION is where you want to go and how you will enjoy the journey, as well as the eventual destination.

The key here is to be open to as many routes as possible, to get you to your place of happiness.

Life is all about setting INTENTION, it is just that sometimes we are not aware of what we are doing. Life isn't a wishing well. You cannot throw a coin in and expect a fairy to deliver your wishes. In reality, life is more like a mirror, which throws back whatever you put in front of it.

Mirror Mirror

If you put out a positive INTENTION, then it will show you a positive situation. Likewise, if you put out a negative one, it will show the same negativity back.

It's a bit like waking up in the morning in a really bad mood, where you expect the day to be a bad one. Then, that's exactly the sort of day you get. Have you ever heard the saying, "oh you look like you got out of the wrong side of the bed"? This is because we believe it's difficult for us to hide emotions, would you agree?

So, start to think about what you really want from life. What do you want to feel like every day, how do you want to be remembered, what do you want to do, who do you want to serve?

3rd Area - MANIFEST

Finally, you have to learn how to **MANIFEST.** So you might be thinking, what on Earth is MANIFEST?

Well MANIFEST is all about putting something beyond doubt or question. It is about making it into a reality. We like to say it in a more modern way ....**MOVE YOUR ASS!**

Book it

It's a bit like when you decide to go on holiday. Can you remember the last time when you wanted to get away from it all? Firstly, you decided where you wanted to go, how long you wanted to go for and who with, and then you took steps to make it happen. That's right, you helped to MANIFEST your holiday.

You may have heard of the concept of vision boards. Personally, we think this approach is fundamentally flawed.

We can guarantee that most people who have one will have a fairly indifferent feeling towards it, and in most cases will not have achieved the life they dream of. To be able to truly MANIFEST, you not only need to use what you can see, but you must also be able to feel your way to the future

If there was no failure in life, what would you do?

When you know how to MANIFEST, you can start to bring your WHY alive.

If you can see it in your mind,

you can feel it in your hand!

The A.I.M is Happiness (Awareness. Intention. Manifest)

AIM is the name of the Programme that we share with our WHYs Women and WHYs Men. After all, I'm sure like me you'd agree that happiness is the aim of life right?

Firstly, for **AWARENESS** there are 2 systems we share with our community, one of these is **The Conscious Realisation Strategy™**

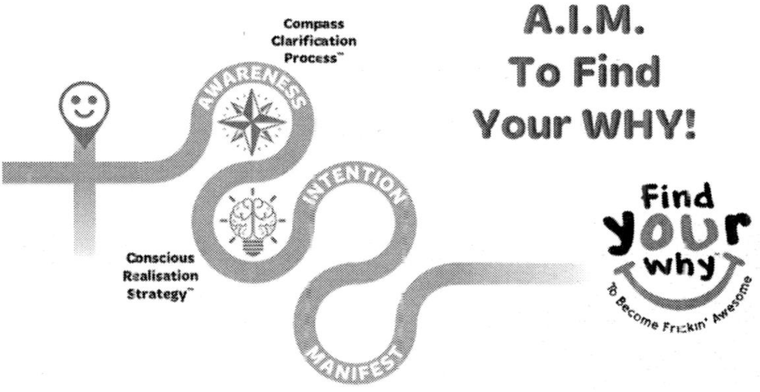

Here they learn how to be conscious about recognising where they are, who they are and what is holding them back. When you learn about these areas you will be able to understand what has happened to you in the past, helping you to shape your future.

In our community our clients learn to share past experiences that can be unravelled with a simple and highly effective process. Experiencing this process allows you to find a positive in every situation.

As the saying goes, every cloud has a silver lining. Accepting that everything happens for a reason, and that life is about winning or learning, allows you to re-write the past and move forward.

With a strategy for turning a potential negative situation into a positive one, you are able to move forward and become the best version of you – right here, right now. Once you are able to consciously realise that you have all the tools you need, you will be able to focus on finding your WHY, to help you to focus on your future.

To help our clients set the right **INTENTION**, we use The **Purpose Realignment Process ™**

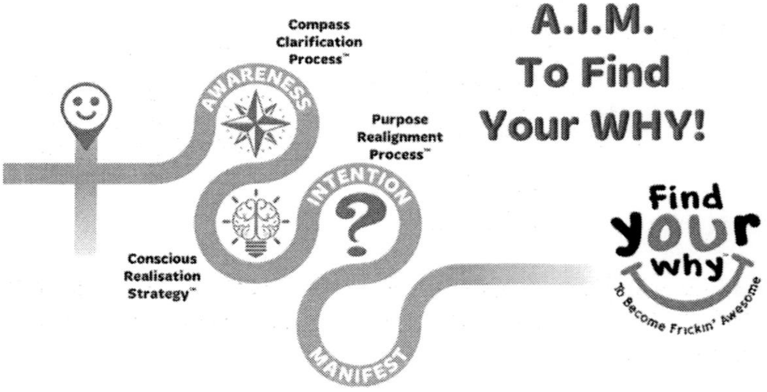

Here we teach our WHYs community how to set an INTENTION, and we show them how they can be open to accepting that the end result will not always arrive by the route they expect. When you are able to master this element, you too will be able to attract what is in alignment with your WHY.

Learning how to be open to success will help you to find a life of true purpose

Our WHYs Women and men tell us that the feeling they have after this process is one of clarity, with a clear crystal 'knowing' that all is going to be well. When you know how to use your WHY to create a life of purpose, you too will be able to feel that sense of quiet reassurance, as you look to a clearer future.

With our **Dynamic Destiny Directive™** our clients see exactly how to MANIFEST into existence the life that they want, that will serve their WHY.

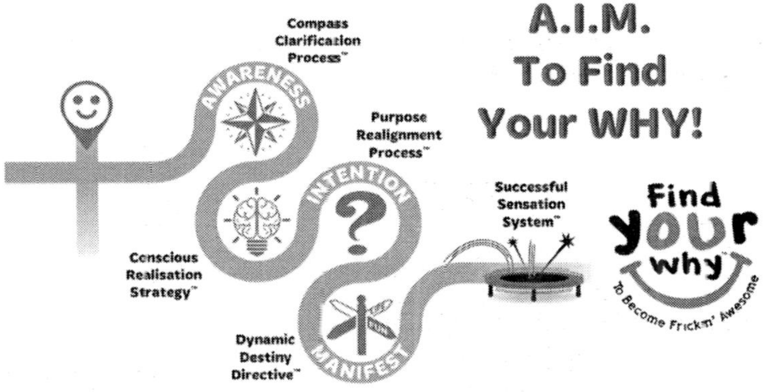

With this system you learn how to make P.R.O.G.R.E.S.S from the initial PLAN to the SUPPORT you need to really make your future one you desire.

There is also an additional process called The **Successful Sensation System™** to help you to manifest.

We would love to teach you how to take the everyday vision board and turn it into a sensational experience, one that will light you up every day as you bring your ideas into reality. When you use your WHY to look to the future, it is as if you are painting a picture of what is already happening right in front of you.

When you understand how to use these tools, you too will be able to A.I.M and create the happiness you desire.

We would love to help you to start your journey, as this is something you should investigate further. In fact you **must** investigate further if you want to choose a life of freedom, and **Find your WHY!**

Keep your AIM Straight

- Be open to AWARENESS

- Set your INTENTION

- Learn how to MANIFEST

- A.I.M for Happiness with your WHY!

AIM

W
A
R
E
N
E
S
S

“IF YOU’RE LOOKING FOR THE RIGHT PATH

YOU’RE ALREADY ON THE RIGHT PATH”

CHAPTER 5

ON YOUR MARKS

To begin any journey, you must know where you are right now.

So what does that really mean?

It's important to take stock of where you are now, so that you can begin your journey towards realising your WHY. Let me ask you, when was the last time you took some time out, just for you?

Maybe you are a daughter, son, sister, brother, mother, father, grandfather/mother, cousin, friend, partner, or possibly you are all of these, and just to clarify these are just the potential roles you have in your private life, let alone your business! So if your answer is "I can't remember" or "it's been a while" then it's no surprise that you may believe that there is little or no time for you!

The great news is that now is the time to make a change, and to put you first. Ask yourself the question, how can you continue to serve and help others if you are not in the right place yourself? A very good example of this is when you go on a holiday flight.

The air hostess will tell you, "In the case of loss of air pressure, oxygen masks will fall from above – please ensure you put the mask on yourself first, before attending to the needs of others." The same goes for your life. How many people can you look after if you're tired, ill, depressed or at worst dead? The answer is none. With that in mind, would you agree that now is the time to focus on you and to have an AWARENESS of where you are? I think you know the answer.

Let me start by clarifying what I mean by AWARENESS. The dictionary defines AWARENESS as having knowledge and consciousness, which means you are able to listen to yourself, recognise how you feel and pay attention to YOU.

In order for YOU to be able to realise your WHY, for YOU to improve YOUR life and for YOU to have more happiness, you need to have Self- Awareness. It's all about you!

Who Am I?

OK I get it Cheryl, sounds easy, but where do I start?

Most people identify themselves by their position in society, their job or their role. However, this is not who YOU are. These are the things you do and the roles that you play. You shouldn't allow the needs and desires of your body, and the emotional and intellectual expressions of your mind, to define your identity. For example, "I'm not very clever and I'm out of shape" or, "I'm just a bag of nerves and I'm never going to amount to anything".

Marion & myself are here to tell you that there is a much better way to contemplate the real nature of your existence and it starts with asking yourself a different question: "Who am I?"

The importance of awareness is about learning how to understand why you feel what you feel and why you behave the way you do. Once you begin to understand this concept, you'll have the opportunity and freedom to change things about yourself.

You may not remember the first time you looked in a mirror and saw your own reflection, however, I am sure you have seen children do this. Their reaction is amazing – a mixture of curiosity, wonder and joy. This is the same as when you remind yourself as an adult that you ARE an individual and that you remember that you are here for a reason. That reason is to live a life of discovery, just like when you were a child.

Once you can see yourself and where you are, you can then begin to get more aligned with your WHY. In turn, this means that you can create the life that you want.

It's impossible to change and become self-accepting if you are not willing to hold a mirror up to your life, does that make sense?

In this chapter we want you to review your current life, reflect and focus on developing awareness. By working with thousands of people all around the world, we have found that there are 8 key areas of your life that you must be fully aware of in order to take control of your own destiny.

By identifying and prioritising these aspects of your life, you will be able to focus on and improve them. This means that you can become aware of how things are for you, what areas you are happy with and what still needs to change in order for you to feel more fulfilled. Then, you can move in the direction that you want to go.

The key is, of course, to have balance across all aspects of your life, otherwise it would be like driving a car with one or two wonky wheels!

Compass Clarification Process™.

The Compass Clarification Process™ can help you to review these 8 areas. So grab yourself a pen and a piece of paper and start to make notes about how happy you are in the following areas:

1. Profession

Are you doing what you love to do? Can you bring love to what you do? Does it support your heart's desire and support others?

2. Partner

Do you have a great relationship? Do you look forward to their company? Do you smile when you think of them?

If you're single, are you mingling, having fun and enlightening those you meet?

3. People

Do you have close positive friendships with others who cheer you on? Are you adding new friends and colleagues regularly? Are you expanding on the kinds of people you meet, in order to expand yourself?

Do you look forward to being with your family or are you holding grudges still? Do you let them be themselves, with no need to change? No one has a perfect family. They don't need to change. We need to change ourselves. They help us practice unconditional love.

4. Physiology

What is your health & fitness like? Do you eat energising food, take regular exercise and relax? How do you treat your body?

5. Play

Are you playing? Really playing? Do you laugh a lot, be silly, and take out your inner child at least once a week? Do you take action to overcome fears (like skydiving)?

Do you take time for leisure either on your own or with your partner/ family?

6. Physical environment

What does your car, home, workspace and wardrobe look like in terms of organisation? Are you happy where you are or do you feel claustrophobic? Take a walk around your house and note how you feel about each room.

7. Personal Development

Are you learning, reading and expanding who you are? Are you exercising your mind? When was the last time you invested in you?

How do you connect to your inner world? Do you experience inner peace and a sense of connection with others?

8. Prosperity

Are you are living a lifestyle you love? Do you feel rich from a financial point of view, as well as an emotional point of view?

Once you have made your notes on each of these areas, take the following 3 simple steps:

Score – We ask my clients on our Lessons On Line Programme to give each of the 8 areas a score out of 10 (10 is fab, down to 1 representing an area that you are not happy with)

Sequence - Now rank the above points in terms of score

Set - This is the area that you want to set an INTENTION to change

We show our WHYs Women & Men how to use the community to help them to stay accountable to make the required change. When you are able to do this, you will be able to go to where you want to be.

Many times we hear from our new community members that they have wanted to make a change but then they lose focus and drive.

We believe that you don't have to figure it out on your own and you don't have to do it alone. **Accountability is the key.** So let me ask you this – who are you accountable to? Who helps you to achieve your goals?

When you have someone who is non judgemental, some one who wants you to succeed then it is like your determination is increased. Try to do it on your own and well potentially it's a recipe for disaster.

Look let's be honest you will already have been successful in some areas of your life and not so in others – WHY? The number one reason is WHY are you doing this, the other is you may feel you are trying to push a big boulder up a very steep hill. The answer to this dilemma is you need support. The Live Love Laugh Lounge and The Man Cave were designed for that reason.

The great news is as you begin to understand the reason WHY you are where you are and WHY you want to change and you start to implement changes you will find your score improves in your chosen area and the knock on effect is other areas improve too, such as your relationships

Throughout this process you will discover new things about yourself, and new truths that will expand your awareness. Think of awareness as a circle. Everything inside and outside the circle is yourself, but you are only able to see and know what is inside the circle.

As you expand your circle of awareness, you will get to know much more about yourself. You'll learn what you are capable of, you'll learn your true potential and you'll learn about the incredible possibilities that the future holds. The more doors you open, the more doors you will discover are still yet to be opened. AWARENESS is the very beginning of your personal growth and development.

Keep your AIM Straight

- Review 8 areas of your life

- Give each area a mark out of 10

- Put them in order of priority

- Take action to address these areas get someone you can be accountable to

AIM

N
T
E
N
T
I
O
N

"Every day, think as you wake up: Today I am fortunate to have woken up. I am alive. I have a precious human life. I am not going to waste it.

The Dalai Lama

CHAPTER 6

GET SET

Now that you have awareness of who you are, where you are and what blocks need to be removed, you can change from an 'I don't want this' mind-set – to one that can bring you more of what you do want. It is now time to understand how to develop clarity of mind.

Without this next crucial element, you may wander around accepting whatever life sends you and perhaps you will never be in a position to use your WHY to its full potential ☺

So, what are we talking about? Allow me to explain:

In order to identify and realise your goals, you need to know how to set the correct INTENTION.

So you might be thinking, what is intention?

Maybe like me, you have heard about an intention with regards to a man's intention to marry a woman (ok so maybe I read too many Rom Com books!) so an intention is a plan of action.

Intention without action is useless, and the same can be said about setting goals. Goals and intentions are equally important, but are also fundamentally different from one another.

The difference between a goal and an INTENTION

Intention is based on your inner world, your feelings, your passion, your values, your purpose and your WHY.

While goals are external, they are the things, situations or places that will bring the desired inner experience.

For example, let's look at the very well-know SMART goal setting process (commonly attributed to Peter Drucker).

SMART is an acronym (I love a good acronym!) for:

Specific

Measurable

Assignable

Realistic

Timed

So a goal using this set of criteria could be, "I will make £100,000 by the 31st December 2017. I will achieve this by hitting all of the monthly sales targets set by my manager."

Would you agree this goal is specific? In terms of monetary value, the answer is yes. It provides clear and measurable targets to hit, the task is assigned to the person setting the goal and relies on the manager setting the targets, it also appears realistic and it is timed for completion by the end of the year. All in all, the five elements of SMART goal setting are used, so it's a good goal, right?

A goal is usually one thing at one point in time. It's very black and white, without any grey area. It's a bit like a game of football – you either score a goal or you don't – there are no ½ points for effort! In other words you either achieve your goal, or you don't!

The problem with goals is that, while moving you towards what you want, they can take you out of the moment and create a feeling that what you have isn't enough, that you haven't quite made it yet, or that you are not enough!

Ask yourself the following question: If your goal is to get from A to B, and the only route you will consider is a straight line, what happens if there is a block along the way? How do you get there? Do you just return to point A feeling like a failure?

When you use intention, you remove the black and white nature of thinking from your mind. You start approaching 50 shades of grey, and I'm sure you know how much more interesting that can be ☺

The reason for this is that intention is not governed by the details of a goal. In other words, when you set the intention, you are allowing for the energy of the Universe to deliver you what you are looking for – in the way that it sees fit.

Now you might be thinking, "HANG ON Cheryl! The Universe delivers? Is this some new parcel delivery service, like UPS or DPD?!" If this is new to you, it might take quite a leap of faith to accept that statement. To be honest, the first time I heard this as a suggestion, my first thought was, "What a load of rubbish!"

Let's review this by going back to the original goal:

"I will make £100,000 by the 31st December 2017. I will achieve this by hitting all of the monthly sales targets set by my manager."

Let's imagine for a minute that you have set this goal. You know that you can't just sit cross-legged and pray for your targets to hit themselves, and therefore you know that you have to take action. However, by being so specific about how this money will come to you and what you need to do to achieve it, would you agree that you have to be laser focused?

Let's consider what could happen if you had 'blinkers on'. In other words, you are blind to the other opportunities that could be around you:

You don't buy a winning lottery ticket?

You are so busy that you don't go and visit an elderly relative that forgets about you in their will?

You don't attend an event where a person was looking to work with someone like you, and wanted to pay a retainer up front?

Now I'm not saying that 'what ifs' are a way to live your life, my point is that when you set a goal so specifically, it leads you to thinking that it can only be achieved in one way. In turn, this leads to you deleting or dismissing other opportunities, that the Universe brought your way.

It is a little bit like looking for the man of your dreams. You could be so focused on a tall, dark and handsome man that you miss out on your soul mate, all because you were focused on looks.

In other words, you can still set a goal as long as you incorporate an intention. Just make sure that you include emotions, your values and that your goal is in line with your WHY. Once you've done all that, then you have to be open for the Universe to deliver you some alternative ways to achieve what you want.

Let's take another look at the previous goal, and turn it into an intention:

"I will make £100,000 by the end of this year. I will do this by doing what I love, having fun, helping others to achieve what they want and making a difference in the world."

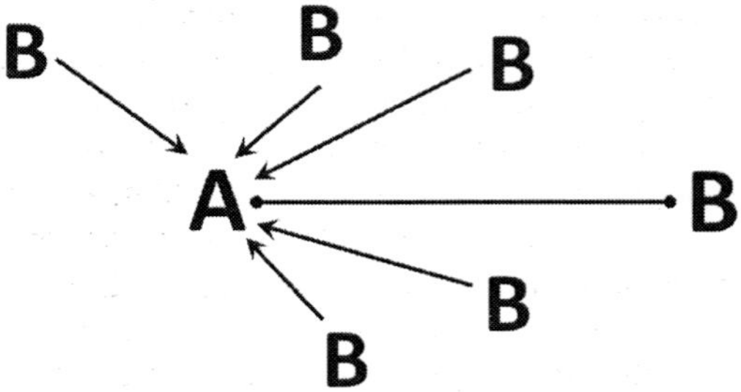

As you can see, intention is the energy behind the goal. It's your desire, your WHY, the power that gives meaning not only to the goal, but also to the experience you have in the process.

Without intention, goals are binary. In other words, they simply require a straightforward yes or no. With intention, you have a motive and a purpose. You open opportunities for future success.

Goal setting is a valuable skill that helps us to stay on track, whilst intention gives us the 'fuel' to get things done. Without goals, you'll have no direction, no destination and ultimately no achievement. Therefore, they are both essential for completing tasks and getting what you want.

A goal is a what, and intention includes the how and the WHY.

Things to consider when planning your INTENTION

The problem is that most people don't know what they want.

Ask them what they what and generally they will give you a long list of – "well I don't want this and I don't want that."

Do you know anyone like that?

What this means is that most of the people you meet will never reach their full potential. They are too busy focusing on what they don't want instead of putting the energy into what they do want. It is a bit like trying to lose weight. Now, I (Cheryl) have to tell you, I have tried just about every technique in the book for this. Whether it's counting calories, eating just protein, different coloured days, stuffing my face with eggs (not pleasant for anyone in a 2 mile radius!!), not eating after 8pm, juicing vegetables, eating natural foods only – the list goes on. However, whenever I tried to lose weight I was only focusing on what I couldn't eat. The inevitable result of this was that ALL the foods I couldn't eat – like chocolate – suddenly became the only food that I could think about.

Maybe you have had a similar experience?

My most successful weight loss came when I was focused on what I wanted, for example to be healthier, so I could be fitter for travelling around the world to connect with large audiences.

I believe it all starts with setting the right intention.

As you can see, success came on the occasions when my intention was set for a higher purpose, one that was aligned with my WHY. By higher purpose, I mean a purpose where you are not limiting yourself to certain outcomes or procedures. In other words, I stopped focusing on the goal. I started to trust that aligning my values, principles and enjoying the experience, would achieve the goal.

In order to have all of this, you need to be able to set a clear intention. When the intention is right, any goal will be achievable.

You might be thinking, "OK Cheryl, this all sounds like it's too good to be true. How does it work?" The answer is simple. By setting powerful intentions, you're BOUND to succeed in realising your goals, because it means that you'll live your life with a purpose. Purpose is what you want to do, and how and WHY you want to do it.

I am sure, like me, that you have dreams, ambitions, goals or aspirations. Things that you want to do or become. But sometimes life gets in the way of those dreams, doesn't it?

It reminds me of when I first started to attend the Professional Speakers Academy. Andy – the founder, was asking for volunteers to help him at his events. I remember Andy was on stage and if you'd been there with me you would have been sitting at the back of the room watching him talking to the audience:

"When you are building a business you must be able to systemise it, stop making it about you the personality and allow it to be taught to others."

Ping! Have you ever had a 'light bulb moment?'

"Hey, I could learn from this. Andy is going to need some help, he doesn't have anyone to deliver his content – it's going to be me!" That was the day my intention was set.

Now I didn't know how, when or where this was going to happen, I just knew WHY! There were no **Specifics**, nothing **Measureable** (other than that I knew I had to learn his content), nothing **Assigned** (Andy didn't even know I had decided this) and it wasn't **Realistic** either. I had never spoken on a large stage, or coached anyone. Nor did I set a date, so nothing was **Timed**. What I did set, was my INTENTION. I just knew that one day I would be on stage delivering his content. I felt as if it had already been achieved.

So, I started to take action. I learned his content, ensured I was around him as much as possible, and then one day – sitting outside the office on a beautiful summer afternoon – I heard the words that I'd been waiting for:

"Cheryl, you have been giving a lot to my company and I'd like to offer you the opportunity to deliver some content at the next event in Johannesburg – are you interested?"

Bingo! This is exactly what I was waiting to hear. My intention and hard work had generated a positive opportunity for me, and there was no way I was going to turn this down! However, I didn't want to say yes straight away! After all, a girl has to play it cool, right?

"Thanks Andy, I'll check my diary and get back to you when I get home tomorrow."

So, fast forward 5 weeks and you find me standing in front of a 200 plus audience in Johannesburg, delivering content, blowing them away…goal achieved, right?

However, 30 minutes later…

"Please welcome back to the stage – Mr. Andy Harrington"

My delivery should have been over 60 minutes. I froze. I couldn't remember my own name, let alone any content!

If you'd been in the room that day, you'd have seen me with tears running down my face as I rushed to the exit, and waited for the taxi to take me to the airport.

Now, here's the thing. If this had been a goal, I would have succeeded. I had stood on stage and delivered Andy's content. The problem is that this wasn't just a goal. This was an INTENTION, and as such I was emotionally involved. My WHY was to serve the audience and Andy, and so as I sat crying in the taxi, I realised how badly I wanted this. I wanted to deliver Andy's content in a way that would inspire them to share their messages of hope and help. I could not leave this one box un-ticked.

I kept my intention alive. Slowly but surely, Andy gave me new opportunities, which led to other opportunities for me to speak and teach across the globe. At the time of writing I have just spoken at four women-only events. The first of these was 'Damsels in Success', where I shared a stage with Ali Brown (Ali was recently named Entrepreneurial Guru for Women, by Business News Daily), so this was quite an experience.

The second event, 'Queens of Life', took place in Poland and was much bigger. I spoke to an audience that was around 2000 strong, and shared the stage with some of Poland's most influential female speakers; as well as Allan Pease, the Author of *Why Men Lie and Women Cry*. I spoke alongside Brian Tracy and Marie Diamond (from The Secret) in the Czech Republic and from that meeting Marie invited me to join ATL (Association of Transformational Leaders), me Cheryl Chapman!! And WHY? Because she said I was inspiring others …ah that's right …my WHY!

So are you ready to set your INTENTION? Are you ready to receive the opportunities that life will show you? Or are you too blinkered to see them?

The good news is that it doesn't have to be this way. Learning how to use the power of intention means that you will know how to make life help you. You can do anything you choose to, and anything you intend to do can be used to achieve your goals.

Why are intentions important?

Intentions give you a framework for you to set priorities. They help you to use your time wisely, and to make sure that you have all the resources needed, in order to manifest your goals. Just by setting and then working towards your intentions, you will be declaring to the whole universe that you are serious about your dreams and goals.

A strong, positive, and energized intention will attract everything that is needed to make it happen.

Have you ever experienced a time when you really wanted something, but when it came, it didn't arrive from where you had expected it? A good example is when you were a child, and wanted a certain gift. I remember one year my sister wanted an 'A La Carte Kitchen', and we hunted high and low for it.

"Oh, those are the must-have toy this year – we are all sold out!" was the regular response. As Christmas Eve approached, my Mum and Dad were at their wits end…then came the phone call:

"Hello, is that Mrs Brooks? Ah good, we'd like to congratulate you. You are the winner of our annual prize draw – you have won first prize!"

You guessed it, an 'A La Carte kitchen'! Now here's the strange thing, none of us could even remember entering a draw. So maybe the Universe heard us calling?

I remember another time when I had very little money and I was desperate. The bills were mounting up, and more importantly I needed food to eat. Just when I felt like I was on my knees, I received a letter from the tax office. I remember opening the brown envelope with the HMRC stamp and wanting to be sick. I read the letter twice – a TAX REBATE! You cannot imagine the relief I felt that day.

So to sum up, intentions can be set for EVERYTHING you do. Before you start to set your own intentions, you should ask yourself the following questions:

What is my WHY?

What do I want to get out of this experience?

What is the result I'm looking for?

How will I feel when this is achieved?

What am I bringing to this experience?

Remember to set the intention, take action and be open to receive.

"Intentions are the breath of your goals, they are the wind beneath the wings of your dreams and only through intention can your goals fly. Intentions fill you with life, with energy and with love. They lift you and remind you WHY you have your goals. Intentions gently nudge you, whisper to you and encourage you. Intentions help you connect to your truth and keep you aligned and in harmony. They help to balance the masculine energy of goals with the feminine energy of holding space so that those goals can be realised. Make your intentions ones that fit with your WHY!"

Anon

Keep your AIM Straight

- Your WHY helps you to set the right Intention.

- Set your Intention and let the Universe supply.

- Set Goals and allow 50 shades of grey ☺

- Do what you feel is right.

AIM

A
N
I
F
E
S
T

“Success is liking yourself, liking what you do and liking how you do it”

Maya Angelou

CHAPTER 7

GO!

Now you can start to create the life you want. Yes, that's right, YOU can create!

Ok, you might be thinking – here you go again Cheryl & Marion. Do you think I'm some sort of creator?

The answer is yes! Just as you have become aware of where you are, and that your goals need to be set with a strong intention, you are well on your way to attracting everything you want in your life. All you need to do, is MANIFEST. As you know, this doesn't mean that you have to take yourself off to an isolated range of mountains in the deepest darkest part of Peru, in search of some incredible witchcraft. Nor does it mean that you can just sit cross-legged on your settee at home – surrounded by candles – chanting in the hopes that a million notes will land in your lap.

MANIFEST is by no means a new word. In fact it first appeared around 1350, and was used to describe something that was visible. I am using the word here in the context of being able to 'see' an image in your mind, and then bringing it into your life. This means that you won't only be able to 'see' it, but also to feel, smell, taste and touch it.

For over 25 years, vision boards have been almost universally perceived as the best means of manifesting. Vision boards are physical (a pin board for example) or a digital version that are filled with images of how you would like your life to look in the future. Creating a vision board is a very simple process, and this is one of the reasons that they are so popular.

So, you might be thinking, what do I do with the board?

Well, one school of thought is to have it with you all the time, in order to make sure you can see it every day, all day. This means that you are constantly being bombarded with the positive images, which serve as an ongoing reminder of what you want. The other advice is to forget about it and let the Universe supply (the good old Universe again ☺)

I personally believe that the whole vision board concept is a waste of time for most people.

"What Cheryl? But hang on, didn't you say that I'm the creator?"

Yes, I did and don't get me wrong, there are many examples of vision board success. These include:

Jim Carrey

Considering giving up on his dream as a struggling comedian after he got booed off stage, Jim decided to pursue his passion. He decided to visualise his success by writing himself a cheque for $10 million, adding a note that read, "for acting services rendered". He told Oprah Winfrey that his 1st film deal for Dumb & Dumber was for...you guessed it – $10 million!

Oprah Winfrey

Tells of how she helped someone else's vision come true, just by using a board.

On the morning of the presidential election – November 4, 2008 – Oprah called New York City radio station Power 105.1 and shared the following story:

> *"I was speaking with Michelle [Obama] Caroline Kennedy and Maria Shriver – we were all doing a big rally out in California. At the end of the rally Michelle said something powerful: "...I want you to leave here and envision Barack Obama taking the oath of office". I created a vision board. I had never had a vision board before. I came home, I got me a board and put Barack Obama's picture on it, and I put a picture of the dress I wanted to wear to the inauguration."*

Lucinda Cross

As a young college student, she made a bad choice that landed her in prison. However, instead of becoming another sad statistic, she chose to learn from her mistake. She chose to take control of her life, and build a better future for herself.

Today she is an entrepreneur, bestselling author, speaker and life coach who's been featured on such prestigious media outlets as ABC, NBC, Black Enterprise, Essence Magazine and many more. She attributes all her success to vision boards and has literally built her business around them.

> "Whether you look at it from a spiritual or scientific aspect, this world is a huge vision board. Everything that's here is because it started as an image someone had in his or her mind. You want to call it a blueprint, or a business plan? Fine. But first, they had to think about it and draft it. So a vision board? It's like selling our own ideas to ourselves."
>
> Lucinda Cross

Maybe you're thinking that I've lost the plot now, saying that I think these boards are a waste of time, but then proving that they work. Let me explain.

For the majority of people, a vision board is just a process that they go through. They collect 2D flat images from glossy magazines, with a selection process that is more akin to a child selecting Christmas gifts from the latest Argos catalogue. In other words, it is more than likely that their selection is based on quantity rather than quality. In turn, this could mean that the emotion attached to these images is about as strong as the emotion used when picking out which toilet roll to use!

With this in mind, 3 years ago I decided to find out how others viewed their vision boards. To do this, I conducted a survey. The results were quite startling.

The participants of my survey were a group of people who were all involved in personal development programmes. Before I tell you what questions I asked, if you have a board, STOP reading now! Go get it, look at it and answer the questions in the space provided:

1) *Why did you create your board?*

2) *When did you create this board & when was the last time you looked at your board/image?*

3) *Where do you keep your board/image?*

4) *Describe the condition of your board/image?*

5) *Describe your board (as if I was on the end of a telephone call, so I can make a picture of your board in my head)*

6) *What do you feel about your board/image?*

7) *What changes would you make if you could?*

Here are some of the more frequent comments that came back; maybe these are the same as some of yours?

1) Why did you create your board?

To attract wealth/so I could focus on my future/to realise my dream.

2) When did you create this board & when was the last time you looked at your board/image?

5 years ago/ 2 years ago/this year.

3) Where do you keep your board/image?

On my laptop/on my wall in my living room/office.

4) Describe the condition of your board/image?

Looks lived in/scruffy/it needs redoing.

5) Describe your board (as if I was on the end of a telephone call, so I can make a picture of your board in my head)

It has a lot of colour photos on it/it contains a lot of positive words & slogans/ it shows images of the life of my dreams/it shows pictures and words to describe the life I want.

6) What do you feel about your board/image & state why?

Sad – this reminds me of what I haven't yet achieved/it makes me feel overwhelmed/I don't feel anything.

7) What changes would you make if you could?

I think it all needs redoing/none – I will wait until this one materialises/ none I don't think it works.

The Common Denominator

Let me ask you a question with reference to the answers received. Do you think these were indicative of the people who had achieved a lot of success with vision boards or not? Let's take a look.

Write down what you have already achieved:

> *"I've visited some of the places on my board. I have done some of the activities on the board. I have a new car/I have achieved some of what is shown on the board, but there is so much more that I expected."*

That's correct – very little success, if any at all.

With these comments in mind, let's review why that could be:

There was no obvious connection between when the board was created, nor where it was kept. Nor was it to do with how many times it was viewed, what the condition of the board was, or even what was on the board itself. I believe the problem with the majority of vision boards is that they rely only on what you see!

Reviewing their answers to how they used the board made them feel sad, and I believe that this lack of enthusiasm is the key! Feeling sad, overwhelmed or even disinterested when looking at what should be your dream, is tantamount to saying, "Don't bother sending me anything good – I don't want it."

Think about this for a moment. If you found the partner of your dreams (maybe they are on your board) but acted like you weren't interested – do you think they would stick around? The answer is NO!

What about the car you've got on your board – have you ever driven it? From my survey, most people hadn't even sat in the car that they had on their board, let alone driven it. Similarly, it may look good to have a large detached mansion in the middle of nowhere, but if you don't like the feeling of isolation – it's not going to be for you, is it? Does that make sense?

How to change the outcome

You must start with your WHY!

What is it that excites you? What lights you up, and what do you really want to happen in your life?

With **The Dynamic Destiny Directive™**, we work with the WHYs women and men to make P.R.O.G.R.E.S.S to help them MOVE in the right direction and with **The Successful Sensation System™** we help them to create sensation boards, so that all of the senses are activated. This means that not only will you like what you see, but you will create a total stimulation of emotions, in order to ensure that you will be inspired by your future.

All of this starts with knowing how to create the appropriate ambience and emotional state.

Using all of the senses allows you to tap into your very essence – so that you can see, hear, feel, touch, taste and even smell your dream. Your dream and your WHY are interconnected. Every time you even think about your dream, you will feel a connection with your WHY. This connection will pull and attract you towards it, like iron filings to a magnet.

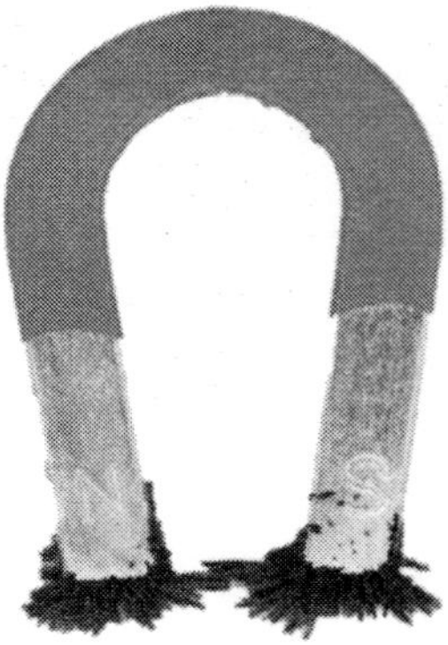

Finally, another crucial element is that you should ACT as IF you already have what is on your board. The reason for this is that the mind cannot separate what actually IS v what is imagined. Now, I know you might be thinking, "Yeah ok, Cheryl, but I don't live in an 8 bedroom mansion by the sea. I don't drive a flash car, so how can I do that?"

Well, it all goes back to this – imagine how you would feel if you did?

That's right, you can still feel the pleasure of having what you want, and of being who you want to be. When you are living with a strong WHY, it is easy to know what that is.

Why? Because you just know that it is in alignment with you. You and your WHY are one and the same.

It's as if the doorbell is ringing with a bespoke express delivery, just for you.

Keep your AIM Straight

- Use all senses to create your board.
- Ensure you are in the correct state before creating.
- Know what you want by aligning with your WHY!
- Live, Breathe & Feel it!

CHAPTER 8

And YOU'RE OFF!

So now you know the three keys to **A.I.M** for Happiness!

AWARENESS, to be able to set your
INTENTION & then
MANIFEST your life of happiness and freedom!

There is one particularly vital ingredient within Awareness that we want to introduce to you. This ingredient will help you to stay calm, in control and congruent to the life that is for you.
The key ingredient is your WHY!

So, you might be thinking, "OK Cheryl & Marion that's great and all I've read here makes perfect sense, but how do I know if I know my **WHY**?"

In this chapter, we will ask you a number of questions that will help you to **Find Your WHY**!

Firstly, we'd like to go back to **The Conscious Realisation Strategy™,** remember this is one of the ways you become aware.

PART 1

One of the 6 steps in this strategy helps you to understand what **STYLE** you are. This means what type of person you are and WHY you are here.

Using a mixture of ancient wisdom and modern day science we can identify which of the **5** styles you are and what your WHY is. Each style has an individual strategy.

To explain this in a bit more detail we would like you to imagine a plot of land.

STYLE 1 walks up to the land and says *"Hey we could build a house on here"*

This is the style we call **The INITIATOR** and approximately 8% of the World are this style.

Each style has an individual strategy. If you are an INITIATOR type of person your strategy in life is to **INFORM.**

Style 2 says *"Hey let me draw up the plans for your house"*
This is the style we call **The ARCHITECT** and approximately 21% of the world are this style.

If you are an **ARCHITECT** type of person your strategy is to **WAIT FOR THE INVITATION.**

Style 3 says *"Hey let me get all the right materials and people for you"*
This is the style we call **The SPECIALIST** and approximately 35% of the world are this style.

If you are an **SPECIALIST** type of person your strategy is to **RESPOND & TEST.**

Style 4 says *"Hey let me build this house"*
This is the style we call **The BUILDER** and approximately 36% of the world are this style.

If you are a **BUILDER** type of person your strategy is to **RESPOND.**

Style 5 says *"Hey let me look at the house once it's finished"* This is the style we call **The NEIGHBOUR** and only 1% of the world are this style.

If you are this type of person your strategy is to **OBSERVE.**

Find YOUR S.T.Y.L.E.

In order to find out which S.T.Y.L.E you are and how to use the strategy all you need to do is go to this page on the website

http://bit.ly/GetMySTYLE

Answer all the questions as acuratly as you can, it will only take a few minutes, and has the potential to change your life. Just as it did for both Marion & me (Cheryl)

Include the time and please state if this is a best guess or actual, and state it in 24hour HH:MM

Once you have completed the questions we will review your answers and then we can share our findings about which STYLE you are and how to use your strategy to help you to:

Find Your WHY! To become (even more) frickin' awesome

PART 2

Getting Closer to Finding Your WHY

Another tool that we use to help find your WHY! is to review your formative years

Question 1

When you were 5 years old

Who did you spend most of your time with?

What did you like doing most?

What did you dislike the most?

Question 2

When you were 15 years old

Who did you spend most of your time with?

What did you like doing most?

What did you dislike the most?

Question 3

When you were 25 years old

Who did you spend most of your time with?

What did you like doing most?

What did you dislike the most?

Question 4

When you were 35 years old (or the closest if you are not yet this age)

Who did you spend most of your time with?

What did you like doing most?

What did you dislike the most?

Summary of Part 2

By reviewing these 4 time periods of your life, you will you be able to see patterns of when you were happy, what you were doing and you'll also be able to recognise the times that you were unhappy – and so now you can begin to identifyinh the things that you need to avoid, the things you need to change and the things you need to do.

Because we believe you are born with your WHY this is an important process and the exercise is best done with somebody else, and will give a clear signpost to what your why is.

PART 3

Leaving a legacy – what king of imprint will you leave on the world.

Imagine that you have been told that are going to die in 6 months' time and that you have to plan your own funeral.

Question 6

Choose a song to play at your funeral that would represent your life.

Please state the title and which artist.

Why are you choosing this song?

Question 7

Choose a headstone from the following images or draw your own:

Question 8

If you could only choose one word for your headstone, which describes how you would like to be remembered, what would that word be?

Question 9

In one sentence, how would you like to be remembered?

Question 10

Choose someone to read your eulogy:

a) *What relationship are they to you?*

b) *Why did you choose them?*

c) *What would they say about you?*

Question 11

Choose one person that you want to write a love letter to. This can be to anyone who is dead or alive:

a) *What relationship are they to you?*

b) *Why did you choose them?*

Question 12

Write the letter to them now.

Question 15

Write yourself a bucket list (20 things you want to do before you die). For the purpose of this list, you should assume that money is no object.

1)

2)

3)

4)

5)

6)

7)

8)

9)

10)

11)

12)

13)

14)

15)

16)

17)

18)

19)

20)

The AIM of this book is to open your mind and to help you find you WHY!. To open up your mind with questions that go deep, potentiall give you some answers - but at the very least help you to becom aware that you DO have a choice!

After reading this far in the book you may find that you now hav more clarity or maybe for you it's more questions; and perhaps you'r feeling a bit discombobulated?

Where ever you are right now - we don't want you to leave you ther without support - ask your self are you curious about how far you ca go? And do you need to take this one step further?

We believe you were born with Your WHY, there has always been seed within you, life may have covered that seed over - and now w know that

"You don't have to figure it out on your own &

you don't have to do it alone"

This is why we would love to invite you to not only get you STYLE bu to also book in a free 20 minute consultation so you know what your own unique STYLE is and how to begin using it!

http://bit.ly/GetMySTYLE

This invaluable wisdom will help you transform the manure of life in to a powerful fertiliser to enable that seed within you to grow and flourish no matter how much life has covered it over.

The reason that your WHY is important is because if YOU don't know what your own passion and purpose are a.k.a. YOUR WHY - then you will end up living someone else's WHY!.

Our **A.I.M** in writing this book is to help you to expand your **AWARENESS**, to clarify your **INTENTION** and to encourage you to **MANIFEST** what you do want into your life.

And now we have A Global Mission

"To Guide 10 Million Disheartened Souls who are at a crossroads, to STOP asking why me? And START saying WHY NOT ME!"

I (Cheryl) feel blessed and honoured to have been guided and supported by many mentors along the way and of course you have already been introduced to one of those, the Female Indiana Jones herself - Marion, so I thought you might like to hear directly from her....

Keep Your AIM Straight

- **Be Honest**
- **Be vulnerable**
- **Write down what comes 1st**
- **Go to http://bit.ly/GetMySTYLE**

CHAPTER 9

MARION

Have you ever experienced a time when your life felt good? I mean really good, as if you'd actually made it?

It's 1998. I'm sitting at my desk in the IT department of Mercedes Benz Finance. Next to me is Chris. He's everything you'd imagine a typical 'computer geek' to be, with his black rimmed glasses and tank top over his shirt (what are tank tops actually for?). We are knee- deep in computer code, and I'm handing over the work I've just completed to him.

"So… umm… Marion, how come you're leaving? You've only been here for 6 months. I mean you are such a creative programmer and you're brilliant at what you do. If you took that job they've offered you, you'd be rolling in it!"

"Well Chris, the truth is, being an IT contractor is only a means to an end. I'm only working here to earn the money to fund my travels. 6 months' work means I've got enough for my next trip. My motto is – I work to live; I don't live to work! - Life's not all about the money."

I can see the look of disbelief on his face – it's a look I see a lot.

I don't expect it to resonate with a guy in his twenties! My travels take me out of the corporate world, and into a world of fascination and new opportunities. It's a perfect mix, and I'm having the time of my life!

Little did I know what would happen to me. Something, which completely changed the way, I looked at the world.

You might be thinking, "WOW what did you do, find religion or a new way of life?"

Well, no it was actually something that literally changed the way I looked at the world.

"Dr… you know you prescribed me with those tablets to help with my thyroid problem? Well I've noticed that my eyes, especially the left eye, have begun to get bigger. It's like it is bulging out of the socket, and because of this I keep getting double vision."

"Ah yes, Miss Bevington, this is one of the possible side effects. It does state this on the leaflet." (Note to self – read the leaflet!)

Now, have you ever heard of the saying, "For every cloud there is a silver lining"? I couldn't carry on with my IT work, as concentrating on a screen with double vision was not practical.

However, on my travels I had an amazing opportunity to help run some yoga classes. You might be thinking that sitting down on the floor cross-legged with your eyes closed is a great way to avoid double vision... EXACTLY!

It was during one of my Shavasana classes (a yoga technique that requires lying on your back) that I had another eye opener!

Barbara rushes in. 65 years old – she's a tall, blonde, ball of energy and has a look of Helen Mirren about her. I remember in her first class how difficult she found it, but she's improved leaps and bounds.

"Marion, I'm sorry I'm late, but I've got something to show you – I can't believe how amazing I feel. Look at my arm!"

As she speaks, she swings both her arms straight up, reaching for the ceiling, "Marion you're a miracle worker!" She hugs me tight as the other members of the class begin to gather around.

""Marion, I've had physiotherapy, so many different types of massage and even acupuncture, and I still haven't been able to do that for over 20 years!"

"Barbara, that is great news for you! OK everyone, settle down, and let's begin."

I can feel the tears beginning to fill my eyes, as a profound sense of pride, satisfaction, fulfilment and gratitude overwhelms me.

Have you ever had a time when you can hear a voice in your head? The voice is loud and clear, "This is what you should do!"

I was filled with a deep sense of knowing, like nothing I'd ever had before.

Now I know, looking back at the time, that this was the beginning of realising my WHY. I'd found what really satisfies me, which is helping myself and others to connect to our authentic essence, by using the body to help feed the mind and soul.

I can hear you saying, "What? All that, just by sitting cross-legged and lying on your back?!"

Well yes, that is one of the core parts of yoga, but what touched me on that day was the essence of yoga – it's so much bigger than the poses. I'm talking about a way of life. I spent the next 2 years in India living and breathing yoga. I trained to be a teacher and yoga therapist. However, I felt like there was more to discover and I knew I still needed to develop my understanding to help heal myself. Yes, I still saw 2 of everything, even opportunities…

Skip ahead to 2009, and I'm in the famous London Moorefield's Eye Hospital, looking around at white-washed medical walls. The room smells clinical.

"Miss Bevington, your condition has deteriorated severely. There's a chance that you could lose your vision, but the good news is we can help you…"

"You must be joking Doc, I've lived like a saint for the past 2 years! How can this be getting worse? Sorry Doctor, what has caused this?"

He looks a bit frustrated, "Well, as I just said, we don't know the cause. Your body is attacking itself."

"So, how can you help me?"

"Well Marion, we'll start you on a high dose of steroids, and a course of nonsteroidal immunomodulators to stop the inflammation. Then you'll have external beam radiation therapy, which will cause cataracts, so we'll do the surgery to remove them. After that, we'll begin the orbital decompression surgery, so we'll pop the eyeball out and shave away some of the bone inside the eye sockets…"

I have visions of eyeballs rolling around on the hospital floor. I'm starting to feel physically sick, and he's still talking…

"Then, to realign the eyeballs, we'll do some strabismus surgery. Finally, we can do eyelid surgery to correct the retraction and then cosmetic surgery, and you'll be as good as new!"

He looks so pleased with himself. I want to throw up! "So… so I need all of this to get rid of double vision?" "Oh, there's no guarantee it will stop the double vision."

"WHAT!!! No way! No way am I going through all of that if it's not going to fix my vision!" The screaming inside my head is drowning out his words

Can you remember a situation when you have heard some news that you just wanted to run away from? I wanted to get out of there.

I don't remember getting home, or ever crying so much when I got there. I didn't want my eyeball 'popped out', but I didn't want to go blind

Surely there has to be another way? I went in search of alternatives. I had many well-meaning friends and family members telling me what I should do, "Marion, have the operations, take the drugs." I became obsessed. I talked about it all the time, and it started to get me down.

Terence (my loveliest brother) seemed to understand. His big blue eyes full of love and his soft voice caressed my ears, "Marion, you must have heard me talk about Máire? She's helped me so much, I think you might like her, so I've made an appointment for you and she will fit you in tomorrow."

So, the next day you find me lying on Máire's couch:

"You know Marion, your body still knows its original template, it's like a blueprint... It knows what it was like before this condition began, and it can get back there if you're prepared to do what's needed."

Template? I'd never heard anything like that before, did she mean like the original software I used to install into the computers?

Máire was exactly what I needed at that moment. She helped me to realise that I am actually in control of my body, my thoughts, feelings and emotions. She introduced me to the Emotional Freedom Technique. This had a powerful impact on me, and so I trained as an advanced practitioner. I began to study more and found META-Kinetics, which uses Kinesiology with a deep understanding of the language of symptoms.

I have since found that my symptoms speak loud and clear, and were established very early in life as a consequence of my perception of the environment I was raised in.

In my quest to heal myself, I have been able to comprehend more deeply the profound wisdom of the body and how to understand what the symptoms mean as well as what to do about them, and it is this that I now share with others, just like I did with yoga.

Like me, many of the people that I started to help were trying to resolve the symptoms and not the cause, the meaning. I found that a lot of the time, most people delete the pain/problem (not you right, just someone you know!).

How many times have you been able to see someone else's problem, when they themselves are unable to see it?

One such example is when I could see something in someone you already know:

Cheryl Chapman

I met Cheryl as a fellow coach at Andy Harrington's Professional Speakers Academy.

I remember thinking, "How fantastic to meet a kindred spirit. A fellow northerner and a straight talker. WOW, she has an amazing ability to see the essence of others. Listen to her! She is so precise with her feedback, not only on the presentation, but she also appears to have laser-like vision of what was blocking other people from achieving their goals."

We started to work together as speaker coaches, and as I spent more time with Cheryl, I began to sense just how much she was holding herself back. She didn't know she was doing this. She would hide her greatness, shy away from it, shielding herself behind an energetic brick wall that helped her to block out emotions. It was clear that she'd experienced some deep trauma, and had learned very early in life how to protect herself. Isn't it strange how you can see something so obviously in others, and yet you still need others to see it in you?

I knew she was a tough cookie, so if I just blurted out what I sensed she'd just shrug it off, probably deny it and I'd never have the opportunity to see her blossom as I knew she could.

Would you agree that sometimes we have to use alternative ways to help someone?

It's like when you encourage a child to eat by pretending to be a 'Chu Chu Train' or an aeroplane, to deliver some kind of vegetable to your child's mouth. Knowing that Cheryl was a supportive and giving person, I devised a plan:

"Cheryl, I need case studies to complete my Master Practitioner in META-Kinetics, would you mind helping me?"

I knew that if I could help her to see clearly what her unconscious limitations were, this would give her the understanding she needed to become even better at helping herself (and others) to blossom and grow.

So, a few days later, there we were. Cheryl was lying on her back, in the living room of my cluttered flat in Angel Islington. I'm balancing my case study sheets on her body, and I can see her state changing. Her breathing speeds up, and her language has changed too.

Wow, I wasn't expecting that reaction. Ok, I'll just write it down, that's interesting... oh shit the papers keep slipping. Never mind, this is fascinating. She's so close to something really important, let me try to see if this is one of her beliefs.

"So Cheryl, does "I have to be careful around people" mean anything to you?"

Oh yes! Eureka! She's crying, so I know she's connecting to this block.

It's such a powerful moment when you bring an unconscious belief into conscious awareness.

"This is really good Cheryl – crying is the best signal we can have right now."

I'm trying my best not to sound too excited or enthusiastic about her obvious distress, but to me, crying like this is like striking GOLD!

"So Cheryl, if you didn't have to be careful – what would you be?"

"Em...em...em... I don't know...what do you mean, Marion? When you say not being careful it s like you want me to stand in front of oncoming traffic on the M1 motorway!"

Handing her another tissue, "Well, what about carefree Cheryl – how would it feel to be carefree?"

"Marion, I don't know, what does that even mean? Carefree – I don't know what it means, isn't the opposite of careful careless?" We agreed that 'mindful' was not too different from careful, but meant being more aware.

Since this session I often witness Cheryl checking herself when she's being too careful, and I'm so happy that I got to share this moment with her. A moment when she began to be free from something that she didn't even know was holding her back.

Have you ever had the feeling that you have more to offer? Often, things that happen to us when we are younger are what lead to these limitations. These are situations where, for whatever reason, you may have needed to stay safe. In order to do this, your mind creates a 'strategy' to keep you safe.

In Cheryl's case – being left alone at 5 years old – staying safe was a good strategy. However, as a woman heading towards the age of 50, it was no longer serving her. It's about refusing to accept your fears. It's about refusing to accept your glass ceiling, and never settling for something good instead of something truly great.

It is only through finding my WHY that I have been able to set my intention, discover opportunities and take steps to create the life I have now. My WHY is to find joy, have fun and guide others to join me. It is about helping them to find their own WHY, and having fun in the process.

Today I have a much clearer vision of life and the condition that was causing the double vision is continuing to reduce over time. I work regularly with Cheryl, with Máire and with other teachers and guides to return to the template, the blueprint of wellness my body still knows.

At a recent visit to the Moorefield's Hospital for an annual check up the tests showed an 80% improvement in the function and form of my eyes, and the doctor was quite puzzled at this since I'd had none of the treatment they'd offered…

"How will you represent this improvement in my medical notes doctor?" I asked curious to know if she would refer to my inner work.

"Well Miss Bevington, I can only state that it is spontaneous remission, I've heard that sometimes happens."

"Really doctor? How do you define spontaneous? I thought it meant instantaneous, and you can see from my notes this improvement has been steadily progressing over the past 5 years!"

As human beings, we are social creatures. Being connected to others, and living as part of supportive and nurturing community, is our innate way to feeling part of this world.

The more you know about who you are, and what your WHY is, the easier it will be to remove the obstacles that hold you back. Now you can focus on what you want from life. You can take steps to achieve your success, and allow yourself to be fulfilled, satisfied and happy!

Finding our individual WHYs allowed Cheryl & myself to realise that as a team, we can help others in a unique way. What's more, we can do so in a way that enables us not only to Live, Love and Laugh every day, but to help others to choose a life of freedom on a journey to happiness.

We look forward to helping you Find Your WHY! and in turn, helping you discover what to do with it!

CHAPTER 10

HOW CAN WE SUPPORT YOU?

Congratulations, you have reached the end of the book!

You might not know this, but by reaching this chapter, you have already put yourself one step ahead of the game. Did you know that many people don't ever buy a non-fiction book after school, and even less actually read them and even less read until the end! Have you ever heard of the phrase "shelf development?" it's a poor alternative to 'Self Development'!

By completing this book, we know that you are already on your way to making positive changes in your life, and not ust someone who pretends that they want to make a change.

If you haven't already completed the WHY questions from Chapter 8, we urge you to do that now. Why would you want to wait? We all need new support & strategies for moving forward, so welcome positive change with open arms. We look forward to learning about you through your answers and connecting with you, and social media makes it easier!

Let's Get Social!

Search for #FindYourWHY!

@FindYourWHY @FindYourWHY_ @FindYourWHY

You can also find us on Youtube and Instagram:

This book is available on Amazon.com – now even if you got your copy from somewhere else we'd love to hear your thoughts and honest feedback on this book and we'd really appreciate if you would post a review on Amazon.

If you would like to be part of The Find Your WHY! Foundation we have the following three options available to you.

How to connect to the WHYs Community

1. Membership
2. WHYs Discovery day
3. Retreats

Membership:

For the WHY's Women we have The Live Love Laugh Lounge™ and for the WHY's Men we have The ManCave™.
As soon as you join you get unlimited access no contract required.

We gather in secret Facebook groups to connect & communitcate. Get access to the Find Your WHY Foundation **Online Lessons** where Cheryl & Marion guide you through The A.I.M to Find Your WHY! Programme, a sereis of short videos & exercises helping your find and refine your WHY!

Regular **Tools, tips and techniques**. Updated every month, we share with you the what the why and the how of all the great tools in our tools kits, to facilitate your continual growth.

Monthly Q&A with Cheryl & Marion During this interactive live broadcast session you will have the opportunity to have your questions answered.

Expert Experience – Experts sharing "how to" based on an elected topic such as write a book, personal branding, marketing, recruitment, social media, public speaking, financial planning, best way to divorce, investing in property, overcoming fears, phobias addictions etc.

WHYs Discovery Day:

ASSOCIATE with likeminded WHYs people face-to-face.
Get into **ACTION** on your business & in your life.
Become **AWARE** of any "shit showing up" & deal with it on the day.
Get **ACCESS** to tools, techniques & support.
Have **ACCOUNTABLITY** within the community.
ACHIEVE steps to align even more closely with your WHY!

WHYs Retreats

The venues we select are always true sanctuarys, oasis of calm. In Marrakech all rooms have their own character, and all have one thing in common – a seductive mix of soft colours, rich Moroccan textiles, and the best craft-work of local artisans. Lusciousness and luxury combined. The atmospheric main house is surrounded by generous gardens and amazing glamping facilities too!

The food is super-fresh and delicious, and the service is unfailingly warm, efficient and friendly. Around the grounds, there are plenty of outdoor spots for relaxing, and there is a lovely courtyard for al fresco dining where you can enjoy the gourmet cleansing cuisine lovingly created by our chefs and nutritionists.

The Find Your WHY Retreats include

- Pre-retreat questionnaire so we can tailor your schedule
- Accommodation, all ensuite, All food and soft drinks
- Daily Find Your WHY teachings
- Daily yoga class & meditation sessions
- Optional Pampering & Therapies Available on Request:
- Deep dive Inner Processing Sessions
- Personal Development take home guidelines
- Final Day New Me – New Life Preparation Session

If you have any questions about Finding Your WHY or if you want to find out more about how to connect and collaborate with us then visit the website www.findyourwhyfoundation.com

In closing, we want to say thank you. Thank you for believing in us enough to read this book, but more importantly for believing in yourself. You are a unique, amazing person and I really hope that our paths will cross again soon.

Please keep us posted on the wonderful things that start to show in your life. I'll leave you with one final story:

When a disappointment becomes a blessing!

By Cheryl:

When I was 7 years old, my parents bought me tickets to go and see The Osmonds in London (they were like the One Direction of the 70's). Donny Osmond was my favourite.

When the tickets arrived, one of them had a star next to the seat number:

"Mum, why is there a star on my ticket?" (Yes it's the WHY question again)

"I don't know Cheryl, I imagine it is a very special seat."

I decided it was the seat that meant I would be chosen to marry Donny.

When we arrived at the event I was devastated to find that the 'star' just represented the seat at the end of the row.

So, why do I tell you this? Well, it reminds me of the imagination you have as a child, and how disappointments mean that you stop dreaming.

In 2014, I flew to Toronto Canada to talk at an event. I saw a sign that Donny and his sister Marie were in town with their Christmas show.

So, off I went to buy a ticket:

"I'd like the best seat you have please."

"Yes ma'am, we have one right in the centre or there is one here on the end of the row, a little further back."

Which seat would you have chosen?

30 minutes into the show, Donny runs up the aisle and stops right next to the seat on the end of the row.

Guess where I was?

That's right, right there.

I stand up and get to hug my idol and then I say, "Donny would you do me the honour of being…in a selfie with me?" (Hey, times had changed in 43 years!)

Here's the interesting thing: I would have never had chosen the end of the row seat if I hadn't had the disappointment 43 years earlier.

In writing this book I also remembered my favourite Donny song was called "WHY"

https://youtu.be/uEZJyfPkWCY

I believe what happens to you in your past is for a reason and in the words of the Osmonds 'Let the reason be LOVE!"

https://www.youtube.com/watch?v=_iVWg5T7fXM

Me & Donny Osmond in December 2014
(ok so the p cture is shit – I was in shock!)

CHAPTER 11

WHYs WOMEN STORIES

Wendy

I am the author of the book Get Out Of your way, the step-by-step guide for entrepreneurs to attract, recruit and retain a winning team. I went to Canada to launch my book with Raymond Aaron – since he couldn't come to the UK! Everything happens for a reason…

I was privileged to meet Cheryl Chapman, one of the speakers at the Women into Power event. I seized the opportunity to be coached by her on the stage and I invested in The Live Love Laugh Lounge (the home of the WHYs Women) and The Find your WHY! Mentoring Programme. The Programme has helped me to develop my self-confidence and has made me look at life in a much more positive way. I dealt with some of those issues from the past that I had held me back.

The Live Love Laugh Lounge is a safe environment to share the highs and the lows and a sounding board for ideas. The WHYs women have been incredibly supportive and I will stay connected with them. Marion and Cheryl have been awesome mentors and when you follow their programme you will be able to achieve anything you want to!

The process has helped me to be clear about my purpose and the direction of my business. Over the years I have worked with several entrepreneurs who were great technicians, but they didn't know how to run their business. So I wrote the book Get Out Of your way, the step-by-step guide for entrepreneurs to attract, recruit and retain a winning team so entrepreneurs could gain an understanding of everything they need to have in place in order to get the right people for their business. That's £2000 worth of consultancy for just £19.99!
Join my club and I will give you all the templates you need to set up your HR systems and processes.

I have a forum where you can share your challenges and get support and advice, we have a blog to keep you up to date with current legislation to keep you right, and you can upgrade to get access to an employment lawyer for when it goes wrong.

I have also designed GEMS, my Great Employee Management System, it's an online filing system so you can keep your employee records digitally and in one place, your employees can log in and update their details, book annual leave, send messages, post notices and record tasks. You can keep track of your team from anywhere in the world as long as you have an Internet connection!

www.getoutofyourwaybook.com
www.lodestonelounge.com
www.mygemsystem.com

Wendy Sneddon

GEMS

GREAT EMPLOYEE MANAGEMENT SYSTEM

Sally

I was introduced to Cheryl and Marion by a close friend and colleague in 2016 and I am so grateful! Initially I just joined the online forum The Live Love Laugh Lounge where I found a lot of support from them as well as various WHYs Women from around the world! They have built a very inspiring community of women. One or two in particular gave me some really great help and advice during a very hard time in my personal life last year. I never thought that this was possible from strangers but it turns out it is!

Cheryl and Marion make a formidable partnership – they bring very different skills to the table, which is one of the reasons their programmes work so well. Both are extremely adept at spotting patterns or behaviours that may not be serving you well in your personal or professional life. One reason I really like working with them is that they help you to focus on important and meaningful things but in a very fun and light-hearted way. It keeps your spirits up despite the inevitable setbacks everyone experiences when moving towards their goals.

Each week, at least one member of the group would be struggling with something and there was always an opportunity to properly talk it over and get some on the spot guidance and support. These two really live their mantra, "you don't have to figure it out on your own and you don't have to do it alone"!

As a self-employed acupuncturist and nutritional health coach, I can feel isolated in my work at times. When I joined their mentoring programme last year, I felt part of a female clan who sincerely had my best interests at heart and really wanted to help me achieve my goals. In fact, I smashed my target within the first couple of weeks, thanks largely to their support and being held accountable! I enjoyed the alternating teaching/support sessions and liked how they made me more mindful in the rest of my life.

I don't think its coincidence that since doing the mentoring sessions, my business has steadily grown. I've just had my most successful month to date since completely starting over 2 years ago.

As a small business owner, something I also really appreciated was being able to pay in instalments. I couldn't have accessed such quality content and experience any other way. It has been really motivating and empowering to witness other women also achieving their dreams. Cheryl and Marion are doing amazing work to change the lives of women (and men) they meet.

If you have even the tiniest smidge of aspiration to do or be something more than you are already and you need a bit of guidance, then I wholeheartedly encourage you to get in touch with them. Together you will definitely make it happen!

Sally Varley Acupuncture & Nutritional Health Coaching
www.hathernacupuncture.co.uk

Angelika

When I met Cheryl and Marion in 2016 I was feeling frustrated I felt alone and I felt that I couldn't do it all by myself and I thought that there was nobody to help. I knew what I wanted to achieve but I didn't have all the skills to do it.

I wanted to learn how best to tell my story to give hope to people and demonstrate with my story anyone can change their life because your past is not your destiny.

My story is not an everyday story, it's not the kind of thing that is spoken about every day but it happens every day!! I'd just like to share with you briefly a bit of my story, if can be help then so can you!

And then share with you how Marion and Cheryl helped me.

I grew up in a very toxic environment domestic violence and being sexually abused from the age of 5 years old by my father. When I was about 8 years old my father planted the seed that when I am old enough be working as a prostituted and make him some money. When I was about 19 years old I attracted the man that into my life that introduce me to the profession of prostitution and I worked many years as an escort girl. Years later I manage to leave him and then some later I stopped working as an escort girl and since then it has been a journey of healing, discovery and adventure of finding out who I really am.

How did Cheryl and Marion help me?

I meet Marion and Cheryl last year in November at an event they were speaking at, I was tears when speaking with Marion and Cheryl I told them I just found you and I can't lose you now, I know you can help me.

Cheryl explained what my options were and how they could help. First I decided to do the 8 weeks online course were we set an intention of what we want to achieve. Which also meant I became a member of the WHY's woman on FB. The Live Love Laugh Lounge is a very supportive community!

I experienced more learning and support on the 3 day WHS's woman retreat.

As a result of that and with the guidance and help of Cheryl I have now a structure in place for my business. I am moving forward with confidence sharing my story on stage and working with people that had similar experiences or just feeling stuck and overwhelmed in life in the form of a Worksop and one to one sessions.

We are a working progress and on our journey to become our authentic self we can be face at times with challenges or patents that we are still running. And with Marion's skills, as Marion helped me to to de-programme the patterns so that they don't have any hold over me anymore and move forward.

Cheryl and Marion have each there unique set of skills which makes an excellent combination with their individual skills to find out what your WHY is and if you know your WHY how to support and guide you to achieve it.

I am grateful for you both having come into my life.

With Love
Angelika Change for Life Mentor
Author and Speaker

Sabrina

I am the mother of 5 children; I call them my fantastic 5. When I first me Cheryl she was helping my daughter and son to speak. Tray-Sean wouldn't speak a he was too shy and extremely withdrawn in public.

Cheryl spent quality time with us and became apart of our family. The children als spent time with her at her home, she never gave up on us,

Cheryl also spotted I was lacking in confidence and she'd always encourag me and created unique opportunities for my family and myself.

The love, encouragement and inspiration she gave us is priceless. Coming int my life way she did and at the time she did literally saved my life. She showe up for me in a major way with calls, invitations, inspiration, friendship love, belief, and deeply grateful for the fact that she has never given up o me until this very day.

I feel honoured to have Cheryl in our lives and as a part of our spiritua family – Cheryl IS the difference that makes the difference.

Since working with both Cheryl & Marion on th Find Your WHY! Programmes I have newfound confidence and have learned to as for help. A year ago I did just that when tryin to get away from an unhealthy environmen and now I have a healthy new home.

I have started to share my message on radi and on stage and the children (now authors and myself have won awards in those area too, being recognised for the impact that w are making on others.

They never gave up on us. They never walked away

Thank you WHYs Women

Kim

I have known Marion for around six years now. She is very insightful and helped me deal with some issues I was having using kinesiology. It is an amazing process because she asks you questions and you make connections you didn't know were there. I had pain in my shoulder, which could be quite unbearable.

I offer anti-ageing treatments that often involve massage. As this helps your blood to travel more effectively to the cells; it also helps relieve stress, which is extremely ageing. I presumed that this was the cause of the unbearable shoulder pain, but I now know although it probably aggravated it there seemed to be a deeper underlying issue.

Fourteen years ago my youngest daughter was born safe and sound and beautiful. Unfortunately, while she and I were fine, my husband, John was taken that very same day into hospital under Section 2 of the mental health act. This left me as his main carer and virtually a single parent to three young children. I hadn't realised when I visited Marion but I was literally carrying this as a burden. Her treatment helped me recognise this and I felt like the weight of the world had been lifted from my shoulders.

I was still a carer and often felt ... often feel in fact ... quite exasperated by John. Marion also recognised this and taught me a tapping technique, Emotional Freedom Technique and I certainly needed a bit of emotional freedom!

I have also watched Marion use this technique to help ease stage fright as part of her SpeakEasy™ programme. It was astonishing to watch the fear just melt away.

It all seems kind of mad but that is fine by me as long as it works ... and it does.

Kim Bridge Wright - Award Winning Author, of
" Forever Young- Living it Forward and Paying it Back"

Gill

If you have read this book all the way though, you are already on your way to a better understanding of the importance of living and working with a sense of purpose.

I discovered the hard way a few years ago, how working or living in a world that does NOT resonate with you is tiring and unfulfilling and will eventually affect your health in a big way.

I was forced to make the changes I needed to take control of my wellbeing by altering my lifestyle, my work and my associates and by finding a way to use my skills and passions that were more authentic to me.

So when I attended the launch of the WHY's Women on International Women's Day in 2016, I was pretty confident that my business as a health and wellbeing coach, using functional nutrition, Pilates, and natural supplementation was a perfect vehicle to achieve my purpose, which is to be able to leave a legacy for my family, my friends and the world at large by addressing our global health crisis with preventative and healing measures.

By then I had known and worked with both Cheryl and Marion individually for over 3 years, and appreciated their particular skills in helping me hone my business, speaking and story telling skills.

However, I was very drawn to the launch event, not least to see how these two very different, funny, and powerful ladies would work together, but also because, although I knew my WHY, I was NOT achieving or attracting my ideal client to my business.

The first thing that happened was pretty amazing. That evening I volunteered to work with Marion on stage.... not knowing what was coming of course.... which turned out to be a great decision, as I experienced a complete reversal in my phobia towards snakes!

I also loved the energy between them both and the positive and inspiring affect they had on the other ladies in the room. So I signed up to their first eight-week online programme

Over the last year, with their support, the collaborative nature of the community they have created and some guidance, focus and straight talking, my business has undergone a whole new evolution.

I wrote my first book, co-authored another, now regularly appear on radios shows and regularly contribute articles to magazines and I have been approached to become a trustee of a global womanhood campaign.

I am honored to be the recipient of both international speaker and author awards.

I have made some amazing friendships from the WHY's Woman community and act as the "resident" health consultant for the growing numbers of women who are drawn to the amazing work that these two very special ladies offer to women who want to step into their power and become Frickin' Awesome.

Thank you from my heart to yours Cheryl and Marion.

Gill Barham

Kerry

I first met Cheryl & Marion at the Public Speakers University, in fact I was one of the coaches when Cheryl attended the training and I gave her feedback! Little did I know how she would play such an important part of my life.

You see, I have been involved in the world of personal development for many years and so I considered myself a positive person who would help anyone. However, the truth was I was wearing a mask.

Before finding my why, I was coasting in the same job for 10 years as an unknown in my organisation. I wasn't happy and knew there was more to life than just surviving.

So when I had the opportunity to see Cheryl & Marion in 2016 sharing "How To Find Your WHY! To become Frickin' awesome" I thought they might be able to help me.

I started their programme and I have to be honest I did my usual – started and then distracted myself and missed a couple of sessions, a repeated habit!

I thought no-one would miss me ....but someone had.

Cheryl contacted me and said she wanted to check I was ok, the truth was I wasn't I felt lonely, lost and life, well that was painful. I wanted to make a change but I just didn't know how.

I still don't know if Cheryl knows how much her contact on that day saved my life.

A year later after using the easy to implement tools and techniques provided by Marion and Cheryl on the course - yes, I completed it!
I can barely recognise my life. The turn around has been pretty remarkable:

- I am now the go to person at work, recognised by the senior managers.
- I beat over 1,500 applicants for one spot on the talent management programme.
- I'm the very first recipient of the WHYs Woman of the Year Award
- I'm setting up my first business
- Writing my first book
- I've fallen hopelessly in love with an incredible man.

I invested in myself, learnt to press my action button, and clear my blocks to move onwards and upwards.

I was able to do this with Cheryl & Marion's guidance and the WHYs Women of super supportive "Live Love Laugh Lounge"

As a direct result I am no longer surviving instead I am living and loving it.

Sometimes the smallest step in the right direction can be the biggest step of your life. As they say it could be YOU!

When I'm asked the investment was worth it, I say it was worth my weight in gold …all 17 stone ☺

The WHYs Women Retreat Marrakech 2017

You don't have to figure it out on your own
&
You don't have to do it alone!